ADVANCE PRAISE FOR *THE MEMO*

"We don't have to fight what was once invisible and unspoken, and we don't have to do it alone, unprepared, or with eye rolls and resignations. In this eye-opening and timely book, Minda Harts puts words to our discomfort and our at-work slights, and gives us solutions and action steps to help secure our professional development and wellbeing. *The Memo* is a must-read for all women of color in business (and for all people who want to do better)."

— Natashia Deón, NAACP Image Award Nominee and author of *Grace*

"Minda Harts hasn't just written an excellent, down-to-earth, pragmatically actionable guide to career success for women of color; she's written a searingly accurate and brutally honest account of what it's like to be Black while working and the countless barriers and microaggressions women of color face. . . *The Memo* is a must-buy, a must-read, and a must-gift—I'd recommend every Chief Diversity Officer and HR department provide copies for all of management to read."

— Cindy Gallop, founder and CEO of MakeLoveNotPorn

"Pursuing a dynamic career as a woman of color in fast-paced, competitive, and often white-dominated spaces no easy feat. But with *The Memo*, Minda Harts has created a comprehensive and compelling guide on how to navigate our careers in spite of the obstacles we face. With lots of insight, research, and a nice dose of humor, Harts gives her reader the inspiration and motivation to go for her dreams—no matter how daunting. This book is a must-read."

—Zeba Blay, senior culture writer at Huffington Post

"For any woman, at any company—even her own. To secure a seat at the table, securing this book comes first."

—Danyel Smith, culture journalist and former editor of *Billboard* and *Vibe*

"An essential and honest guide to taking our rightful place in the C-Suite with tangible solutions about how to break barriers and pave a new path for ourselves—and the next generation."

—Jamia Wilson, director and publisher of the Feminist Press

"Harts provides a necessary guide written from and to women of color . . . followed by a much-needed wake-up call for her white readers, in how—and how not—to be an ally. The result is a much-needed new perspective on an overwhelmingly white genre."

—*Publishers Weekly*

THE MEMO

THE MEMO

What Women of Color Need to Know to Secure a Seat at the Table

MINDA HARTS

SEAL
PRESS
New York

Seal Press

Hachette Book Group

1290 Avenue of the Americas, New York, NY 10104

www.sealpress.com

@sealpress

Printed in the United States of America

First edition: August 2019

Published by Seal Press, an imprint of Perseus Books, LLC, a subsidiary of Hachette Book Group, Inc. The Seal Press name and logo is a trademark of the Hachette Book Group.

The Hachette Speakers Bureau provides a wide range of authors for speaking events. To find out more, go to www.hachettespeakersbureau.com or call (866) 376-6591.

The publisher is not responsible for websites (or their content) that are not owned by the publisher.

Some names and identifying details have been changed.

Print book interior design by Jeff Williams.

Library of Congress Cataloging-in-Publication Data has been applied for.

ISBNs: 978-1-58005-846-9 (hardcover); 978-1-58005-845-2 (ebook)

LSC-C

10 9 8 7 6 5 4 3 2 1

Dedicated to my Mom, my first best friend.

"Our gifts belong to us."

–NTOZAKE SHANGE

CONTENTS

PREFACE

I N 2012, I was living in Los Angeles and trying to cope with the death of an unarmed black teenager named Trayvon Martin. I worked in a predominantly white environment, and no one in the office was talking about his death. Up until that point, I had never seen myself as an activist. Not in a Rosa Parks type of way. I did launch a grassroots campaign called "Broke or Vote" to get more middle-class and working-class people to the polls during President Barack Obama's second campaign, but that was the extent of my activism. I guess you could say I had been going through life with my head down; black women are often told to do just that, especially in the workplace. Even though I saw bias all around me, I knew I could never rock the boat and speak out on it. I mean, who would care or do anything about it? But something about Trayvon's death touched me at my core. Maybe it's because I have two younger brothers and plenty of black male cousins, and I know how easily one of them could be in this same situation. I am sure his death caused many of us to question how we could help. Then out of the blue, one of our administrative assistants asked me to join her for a march that was taking place in honor of Trayvon. She also asked if I wanted to buy an oversized hoodie that had Trayvon's face on it, and as she walked away, she said, "I figured you were the only one I could ask." Now I can only speculate on what she meant, and I joked around later with friends about this white woman giving me a Trayvon Martin hoodie—did she do that because I was the only black woman in the office? We (people of color) always question why "others" do some of the things they do. But I know she meant well!

Now you're probably wondering what this story has to do with *The Memo*, but it has everything to do with how I came to find my voice in advocating for women of color. I ended up going to that march and there were tons of white men and women marching, and it hit me. We need to be on the front lines of our own issues. I still wasn't sure what that meant for me, but I was constantly questioning where I fit into this advocacy equation. Fast forward a year and some change, and I was working on the East Coast. The verdict was out: George Zimmerman was not guilty. I cried that night as if I could feel the pain of Trayvon's parents. And mixed in with those emotions, I was going through my own personal hell of working in an environment that was less than equitable. It was on that night that I realized I had to do something. My advocacy wouldn't be on the front lines with the Black Lives Matter movement; my advocacy would be inside the workplace advocating for women that looked like me. I had to fight systemic racism in a way that was authentic to me and that would allow me to use my expertise. Mellody Hobson would later use the term "corporate Kaepernick," and I felt like I was something like a Kaepernick; addressing the inequalities that we often are scared to address. I had no idea what I would do or what it would look like, but I knew I had to do something!

Around the same time, *Lean In* by Sheryl Sandberg came out. I was heavily into professional development and consuming every business and self-help book I could get my hands on. After reading countless books, I realized that race or intersectionality was rarely—if ever—a topic of conversation. And the books I was reading and the content I was consuming were being produced by white women. It started to become very problematic for me to never read about the experiences of women of color at work. We were completely left out of most narratives. So I decided my form of advocacy would be to create a platform that served our needs and highlighted the challenges women of color face in the workplace. Again, I had no idea how that would look and wouldn't until 2015, when I was forced to write a business plan for my unnamed company. All I could think about was Shirley Chisholm's quote, "If they don't give you a seat at the table, bring a folding chair." And on a train ride from Washington, D.C., to New York City while listening to a Drake song called "Trophies," through my earbuds came the lyrics "Did y'all boys not get the memo?" And that line hit me like a ton of bricks—the workplace has not gotten The Memo: women of color deserve a seat at the table, and we are coming for those seats! It took time to build, but in the fall of 2015, I launched The Memo newsletter, and from there my business grew to include career boot camps, a speaker's series, and an annual awards event. My activism was kicked off by Trayvon Martin—his death showed me that there was advocacy inside me waiting to come out. I went from someone who was fairly shy at times to someone speaking about the inequalities women of color face and challenging the "lean-in" doctrine. And in those days, Sheryl Sandberg could do no wrong, so most white women just looked at me sideways, but my message was resonating with women of color all over the country.

I have to admit that I was scared to launch The Memo. Imposter syndrome reared its ugly head. I wasn't sure if I was the one to continue carrying this mantle of those who came before me like Ida B. Wells, Essie Robeson, Addie Hunton, and Maggie Walker. But as my friend Lolly Lynette said one day during a text conversation, "They would be proud." The funny thing about advocacy is that people will try to tell you what you're doing won't work, and they won't see your vision. I had countless people tell me that I shouldn't start my company because there already were career platforms for women. I was most discouraged by white men, who pointed me to companies like Levo League, The Muse, and countless other platforms run by white women, at least in part because they were investors in those companies. They couldn't see that our missions were very different at the core! It made it hard to raise money because no one wanted to invest in women of color in this way. There were days I would be on the phone with my cofounder, Lauren, and we had twenty dollars in our business bank account. And even though we continued to bootstrap our company, we knew we had to get the word out to more women of color so they wouldn't lean out of the workforce due to isolation, lack of opportunity, and bias. I am so happy that Lauren never gave up on me and the vision. I know our journey hasn't been easy, but it has been worth it.

Now, I bet you're curious how The Memo went from a Drake song to this book you are reading or listening to. I'm glad you asked! Let's go on a mini-journey to how we arrived at this point. Sometimes I laugh and wonder if God had this in his plans the entire time, and he chose me not to show me the road because he knew I might have turned back around. I was not the person I am today or half as vocal five years ago—I can honestly say it's been a metamorphosis. My curiosity was larger than my fear, and I didn't want to see another woman of color crawl through her disappointments in the workplace and have no one ever acknowledge them! I was tired of the workplace being separate and far from equal. I was exhausted from the labels and the BS. And, I know we need to make more people aware of how difficult securing our seat at the table can be—I had to write my story and tell the stories of other women of color. And even though most people don't want to admit it, we can't talk about advancing women of color, or the future of work for that matter, and not address race and the history of this country.

When I looked back, I realized I have been writing poetry since I was in grade school, yet I never saw myself as a writer. I won a Martin Luther King Jr. Award at Macedonia Baptist Church during black history month for a poem I wrote. And after college, I wrote a Christmas play that was inspired by Beyoncé in the movie *Fighting Temptations*. (Let me warn you now, I am a huge Beyoncé fan, and this book will have you swimming in all things Yoncé.) And even after writing tons of content for our Monday newsletter, I still never called myself a writer. Some people have daydreamed their entire lives about writing a book. But I had never considered their entire lives dreaming big enough! Then I realized I wanted to write a love letter to women of color. I needed to take advantage of this opportunity to tell our stories and shine a light on the fact that not all women experience the workplace in the same way. And I wanted to write a book that would give white people insight into how they have played a role in our barriers to entry.

I don't have all the answers, and I feel honored that you would go on this journey with me to address the issues that many of us have faced or will face in the workplace. Let *The Memo* sound all the alarms and break any glass that has held us back. At times you might laugh and at other times you might cry because our road traveled has not always been easy. The current system is broken, and it will take all hands on deck to reassemble a table that did not originally have a seat for us. But the good news is that this is our story, told by us! Time to Secure Our Seat at the table and give everybody The Memo . . . let's go!

1

THE UGLY TRUTH

N 2013, I read this book that I had heard so much about. There was finally a book for women that would address what it's like for us in the workplace. It was a huge topic of conversation at the water cooler and at dinner with friends. I couldn't go anywhere without hearing about *Lean In*. Companies across the country even started lean-in circles—groups of women who would come together to discuss goals, challenges, anything of the sort. It is safe to say that it was something like a revolution, and I wanted a piece of the action. I had never seen anything like it! *Lean In* sparked a national conversation. Who the heck is this Sheryl Sandberg lady? I thought. I wanted to shake her hand, and I hadn't even read her book yet. As an avid reader of everything from *Real Housewives* memoirs to James Baldwin, I went to get my copy and started plowing through it.

But after reading, I felt confused. And I didn't feel the way many of my white counterparts did. They felt inspired and empowered, you know how white people do, that Hell Yeah! type of energy. Something was missing for me. This new manifesto was encouraging women to speak up. But black women and many working-class women were already doing this, oftentimes in the face of opposition and where there was no room for advancement. I remember wanting to shake the book in the hope that some advice would fall out that addressed the differences faced by women of color in the workplace and how leaning in isn't a *wash, rinse, repeat* equation for us. If I leaned in any more, my face would be on the damn table. Listen, many of the book's basics like networking and advocating for yourself—all great advice. But networking and advocating for yourself look very different at work for women of color, especially if you are the only person of color in the office. And not to mention, if you didn't graduate from an Ivy League school like Sandberg, your network might look different. What does this white lady know about struggling at work? She wrote a career book from a place of privilege, and she already had a seat at the table, so leaning in was easier. Her feelings were valid, to be clear, and I don't want to take that away from her. But while she was pissed about not having a prime parking spot during her pregnancy, black and brown women were "leaning in" with systemic racism that prevents us from using our voice to speak on subject matters like support for working mothers or the wage gap, because we often aren't yet at "the table." Imagine me busting down Sergey Brin's door at Google and demanding new workplace policies. He would probably call security. Who is this crazy black woman leaning in!

And equally as disappointing was the fact that most white women didn't even have enough emotional intelligence to realize that this book didn't touch on race and the inequalities that women who look like me face, yet they wanted everyone to read it in the women's book club! Lorraine Hansberry said it best, "The whole realm of morality and ethics is something that has escaped the attention of women, by and large. And it needs the attention of intellectual women most desperately." The fact that Sandberg's entire book was written from a place of privilege absolutely floored me. Call me cynical, but I would have liked to face some of the problems she wrote about! Instead, I was battling two white colleagues who were making work less than bearable for me, and I was the only black woman on our team. Let me tell you another part of the struggle: never reading about women in business who look like you or reading statistics that include you. So yes, you have no idea how disappointed I was after reading *Lean In*. I was hoping this career book would be different from the others, that I would finally feel seen. It was just another career book by a white woman that hit the bestsellers list, talking about white women sh—! I placed this book next to the countless career books written by white women like *Girl Boss* by Sophia Amoruso and *Nice Girls Don't Get the Corner Office* by Lois P. Frankel that ignore my experiences in the workplace, give no thought to race and access, or add little side notes so they don't forget about the black girls (an afterthought).

I know I might get some flack for stating what is already obvious to women of color, but here is some breaking news: we are no longer satisfied with reading your white women tales from the career crypt. Our experiences are different, and it's time we discuss them. All women don't have the same experiences in the workplace; yep, I said it! And even though we have hit movies like *Hidden Figures*, it doesn't feel good to get treated like a hidden figure at work. Just because white people might not see us doesn't mean we don't add value to the bottom line each day. And just because we don't hold many leadership positions like our white counterparts doesn't mean we don't have the capacity to lead. Women of color are like the heart and kidneys of the workplace—you can't function without us! We don't need more career advice from white women telling us what we need to do to advance our careers if we just work a little harder or how it's the white man's fault. Those are just more sad love songs that I can't take hearing any more. Well, as far as I'm concerned, Time's Up on the narrative that all women experience the same sh—at work. Yes, "women" as a whole do not have parity, but often when we discuss women in the workplace, it's white women most folks are referring to. It's a sad fact that women of color are supposed to always buy these career books and pretend it's all good! I want to know when was the last time Sheryl, Sophia, or Lois read a career book about a woman of color and her experience at work? In the famous words of comedian Katt Williams, "Don't worry, I'll wait!"

I had to finally come to terms with my bitterness and make it better—that's what I'm doing with this book. Career solutions for black and brown women are not one size fits all, and I would like for people to stop acting like they are. I think it's safe to say that we are fed up as a whole and tired of fitting into your box; it's time you heard about what "leaning in" is like for women of color. We want to read about our workplace experiences and nod our heads up and down. And we sure as hell ain't taking any more advice from a white woman who claims to empower women when women of color make up less than 5 percent of the workforce at her company and then publicly states how she is struggling to find black and brown women to put in leadership positions and hopes to do better next time. Do better *now*! I guess I've proved my point: Lean-ing in doesn't work the same for us, and we don't need Sheryl speaking for us anymore; we will take it from here, sis!

Now I know what you're thinking: sounds like another an-gry black woman. Well, the National Center for Educational Studies says that I am part of the most educated group in the United States, and yet there seem to be permanent barriers in place to prevent women like me from advancing in our careers. You would be angry too, boo. Our good friends at Leanin.org put out a report in 2018 stating that women of color hold less than 11 percent of management roles, less than 8 percent of senior management roles, and less than 4 percent of executive roles in US Fortune 500 companies. How would you feel ob-taining all of this education and still not having access to more leadership opportunities—and sometimes we aren't even part of the interview process? How would you feel if you never read or saw your stories told in the workplace? Not in *The Help* and mammy type of ways; we've seen enough of those stereotypes!

It is time to dispel the myths that all things are created equal at work, that if you just work harder, you can get your seat at the table. Well, black and brown women have worked hard since we stepped foot on American soil, and some are the hardest-working women I know, but "hard work" has not done us any favors! Only a select few, and I mean select (less than 4 percent), have reached the leadership level of a Fortune 500 company. And that's just one of the ugly truths. We have checked all of the boxes that we were told would get us ahead, and guess what? Not much has changed! There is no shortage of black and brown talent that could fill those leadership positions. Women of color make up almost 14 percent of the population, and companies can't seem to find one or two women to recruit, retain, or advance? The lack of representation in the working world at the highest levels is unacceptable. And, let's be clear, it's not because there aren't any successful black and brown women in business. We just aren't being elevated to the top, and our experiences are not being amplified so that we know we're not alone. We want to read about the experiences of women like us. It's one of the main reasons writing *The Memo* was important to me: for us, by us!

And to add insult to injury, most of the successful businesswomen that we read about are white. How can you be what you can't see? As much as we know about Sheryl Sandberg and Marissa Mayer, we should also know about the Stacy Brown-Philpots and Ursula Burnses of the business world. Ask five white women to name five successful women of color in business and I guarantee they couldn't, but ask five women of color to name five successful white women in business and they could even add one for extra credit. Thank God many of us had Mary Jane Paul, Annalise Keating, and Joan Clayton, fictitious black women to look up to on television, or we might not know what a professional working woman of color who wasn't a reality TV star looks like. I believe one of the main reasons the movie *Black Panther* was a hit is that people of color finally had something for us, by us! And the ripple effect this movie will have on young girls who saw the character Shuri will catapult hundreds of black and brown girls into science, technology, engineering, and mathematics careers. There is power and beauty in seeing what you can become!

I spent much of my career in corporate America and the nonprofit sector as the only black woman or one of a few women of color in the companies and organizations I worked for. And I had no mentors or sponsors that looked like me. For years, I started to question if women of color even wanted more out of their careers because I never saw any in my industry. And my experiences of being the "only one" were happening in even more isolation because I had no one to talk to about them. I spent many years of my career wondering if my coworkers were being racist and preventing me from moving forward or if I was making this up in my head. If someone said something inappropriate to me, then it was up to me to be strong and not take what they said out of context. "Oh Minda, you know I didn't mean any harm!" The last time I checked, no one was cutting me an extra check to be "strong" at work! My white counterparts would never understand the isolation I was experiencing. This is just one of the many forms of mental gymnastics that women of color go through at work because no one ever bothers to address our experiences. Showing up every day as the minority has never been easy, but as women of color we keep pushing forward and believing that if we work harder, maybe a seat will open up for us. As I said before, we can no longer subscribe to this outdated mindset; we are ready to build our own tables, sit at yours, and create our own place settings if need be. The bottom line is, we are coming for those seats, like it or nah!

What They Won't Tell You

There's so much I wish I would have known before I entered the workforce and worked day to day for companies that weren't always thinking about ways to include me at the table. Maybe if I had career advice geared toward women like myself, I would have handled hard situations much differently. It's not just about being the only one, it's about owning our own narratives, calling out the bad sh—, and thriving at work, not just surviving! You know, stuff like office politics. Those unwritten rules that no one tells us about. Being a woman of color in predominantly white spaces is not an easy feat. I often had to replay the old skool song by Mya and hum, "I can't / let you / get the best of me!" because each day was a struggle.

For so long, I tried to fight the fact that there are rules to this getting ahead thing. No one sat down with me and said, "Hey, girl, this is how you play the game. This is how *they* do it, and this is how *they* win." Nor did anyone tell me, "Hey, girl, hey; you will work side by side with them for over ten years, people you thought were friends; one day they will throw you under the bus to save themselves, and you will be left to fight back alone." I graduated from college, naively thinking, *I have my degree, I will make a crap ton of money, have a corner office, and buy those Gucci loafers I've been eyeing.* What I found out is, I should have negotiated my first salary because I could barely afford to buy shoes at Payless. I didn't even know there was something called "office politics." Lastly, I didn't know I would need someone in my corner to help me along the way. Some call those people mentors or sponsors—I like to refer to them as *work-wives* or *work-husbands.*

Oh and the workplace labels! I wasn't aware that some of my future coworkers would label folks that look like me as the *angry black woman, feisty Latina,* and *docile Asian.* Who came up with these ugly—not to mention racist—terms, because I sure as hell didn't sign off on this company memo. Attention, Human Resources: please send out a memo on day one informing us about all the workplace BS we could potentially be up against as people of color. I definitely could have used a heads up! And, to be honest, I kind of blame the colleges and universities because they didn't prepare us for overcoming microaggressions, imposter syndrome, or biases. I guess they wanted the inequalities we'd face at work to be a surprise!

Ask About Me

I graduated from high school early and spent almost two years at junior college because my high school advisor said I should. He steered many of us students of color to the community college and military routes, yet encouraged the white students to apply to four-year colleges and universities. Being a first-generation college student, I didn't know my options. I wanted to attend New York University, the University of California at Berkeley, and Fisk University, but was told I wasn't ready. I came from a low-income family, and I didn't know what resources were available to me. I found out that no one is going to save you and tell you what you need to hear. Eventually, I realized I was my best advocate, and after my short stint at junior college, I applied to a four-year university. I learned that I had options just like the white kids do, even if I had to discover them on my own. Don't get me wrong; there is nothing.

shameful about a two-year college. My point is that there are paths we can take if we just know they exist. *What if my high school advisor had helped me with my college applications? What if he had told me that if I want to be somebody, if I want to go somewhere. . . .* Bottom line is, he didn't. Good thing I figured it out on my own! And the last time I checked, too many students of color are still being farmed out to the local community college.

Racial Growing Pains

After college, I entered the workforce like most newly minted graduates; excited to be out on my own and prepared to live out my dreams. But before I could "live the dream," I had to go through some racial growing pains that had me questioning my sanity and how long I could last working with white people. Not because I didn't like them, but because of the problematic sh— that comes out of their mouth a few times a day. I vividly recall two examples of this kind of nonsense as if they happened yesterday. First, I remember picking my boss up from the airport before a big client meeting. It was a Sunday afternoon, and I was wearing a summer dress, sandals, and a fresh manicure. The color was burnt orange. My boss and another colleague hopped into the rental car. About ten minutes down the road my boss joked, "You people love your bright colors." He laughed like it was comedy night at the Apollo, and my other male colleague chimed in with his agreement. I will never understand how my nail color turned into a fifteen-minute conversation on how black people love bright colors. Mind you, this was from their limited perspective on "us people." I laughed it off, despite being internally annoyed and thoroughly confused. I happen to like burnt orange! The last time I checked, Crayola didn't make a special edition of bright crayons for black people. I was too young and not well-versed enough to address my boss in a manner that would make this a teachable moment for him. I regret letting him get away with such a lame stereotype.

Soon I began to think this must be normal white workplace behavior, because things like this came out of his mouth on a daily basis. Perhaps if I had said something, he would never have made another woman of color feel bad about her bright colors again! But I didn't know if I could or should address occurrences like these. I would tell myself that he didn't mean any harm so that I could push through my workday and not internalize what he really meant (which was to make me feel different and ostracized). Women of color are not encouraged to speak out on situations that involve race, and when we do, HR isn't always the most welcoming. Imagine if you worked at a company like Uber and you did go to the HR person and she happened to be one of the main people terrorizing you. Then what the hell are you supposed to do? That's just one example of having black and brown skin and not knowing who might advocate for you or whether today will be the day you are left out on the island alone. Being a black or brown woman at work shouldn't be so hard, but the powers that be don't have anyone to keep them accountable!

Later down the road in my career, a female colleague continued to refer to me as the "black girl." Since when is it ever okay to call a thirty-something black woman a black girl in a professional setting? It never is! This is not a remake of "Ebony and Ivory"! By the time that happened in my career, I knew how to play the game and was confident enough to handle the situation with poise and professionalism. But even as I addressed my colleague, I was nervous about the possible backlash that might arise because of finally standing up for myself at work. I doubt she will ever refer to another black woman as a girl again. There are things you don't find out until you experience them. There were plenty of times I wanted to run out of the office and cry, but I had to suck it up and remain strong. And there was one moment in my career when I got tired of being "the strong black woman" and I broke down in tears in my manager's office. I mean, where do the broken hearts of women of color go when we can't take it any longer?

We Gon' Be Alright

I spent over two decades working in environments where I was the only woman of color in the office, and I learned *a lot*. I learned how to play their game. I learned how to play it so well, you could fly me to Vegas and let me deal the cards. White people are so good at this imaginary game of life and continue to get ahead, mainly because they don't have systemic issues that beat them down each day, so they are free to spread their wings and fly! I am not mad at them. I scouted, I studied, and I implemented. I wanted to get ahead, but it would take more than a simple Google search to find the rules to this game. No one sends the black and brown community a care package with the tools we need to thrive in a workplace that isn't designed for us to advance. Some of us figure it out, some of us muck it up for everybody else, and some want to be the "only" person of color and decide never to share the secret sauce. I know what it takes, and I am sharing the wealth. Jesus loves all his children and wants us to win like DJ Khaled, but it takes a particular art. You have to finesse this thing like your name was Bruno Mars. You can't show up to work like Sheneneh from an episode of *Martin* and expect to get promoted. It takes self-assessment and self-investment. It also takes some guidance, some advice from those who walked the path before you.

Now What

You have taken the first step by buying or borrowing or downloading this book (high-five). I want you to read it like it's your daily business devotional. Whitney gave you "The Greatest Love of All," Beyoncé gave you "Formation," and Oprah gave us everything! My gift to you is this how-to memo to advance, get money, and secure your seat at the table that's right for you or create your own. There is a responsibility that each of us has once we enter the room and sit in our seat, and that's to fill the table with other women of color. Success is not a solo sport. I want you to know we have choices! And I can't speak for all women of color and our experiences—hell, I can't even speak for all black women—but what many of us have in common is that we are a marginalized group in the workforce. I see you, I hear you, and I am rooting for your success! I want to see more women of color crushing it in the boardroom, leading at the head of the table, and stacking more coins than a slot machine. I don't want anyone to call you an angry black woman ever again. We don't have to play into a narrative that they created about us. It is time we create our own workplace narrative about who we are and who we want to be at work. I want those words to change to a confident woman that knows how to get sh— done. I want you on the *Forbes* top whatever list. You deserve it. You can have it.

First, we have to make a commitment to one another—and I have two rules:

1. As you read this book, take notes! I will share career stories of my own and other women of color that I have met along the way. Learn from us and add these tools to your personal tool kit.

2. Don't take sh— from anyone. You worked too hard to lean out now!

Our careers are serious business. We can no longer ignore the annual reports year after year reminding us there are no women of color in leadership positions and there is little to no action from companies to retain or advance us. And we can no longer ignore that there are inequalities that have kept us from securing our seats! I would be remiss if I encouraged you to ignore the strain between white women and women of color in the workplace—you bet your bottom dollar, *The Memo* will address that too! It is one thing to call yourself an ally, and another to show up for women of color when it truly counts!

Additionally, there's some work that we can do to invest in our skills so when we take our seats, we will be ready to lead. Skills like self-advocacy and how to build your network. You might have graduated from a top school in the country or received a GED, but the short and long of it is, you still need to know how to get ahead. Your background will only get you so far. These are just some of the ugly truths along the way. There are biases, but we don't have to be victims! There are mean girls at work, but we don't have to turn into them because of our workplace broken hearts. My prayer is that you walk away knowing what is possible for you and your career—as a woman of color!

Let's be honest, white people have done an excellent job of building and leveraging their networks. They have done a great job of promoting their peers. They have a certain confidence that when they enter a room, they own it. And they have done a horrible job of being inclusive! Often we don't see diverse representation in the workplace, and that can hinder our ability to advance. Early in my career, I worked my butt off hoping someone would take notice and my work would speak for itself (also known as expecting a system of meritocracy). Sometimes the right people will take notice, and other times they won't. You must learn to be your own advocate. If we don't know how to promote ourselves and create strategic relationships, we may end up in the basement like Milton from the movie *Office Space.* Once I learned how to leverage my voice and speak out on the issues that only women of color face in the workplace, I felt like one of the NFL players taking a knee during the national anthem. I began my advocacy because I couldn't bear another woman of color graduating from college and entering a corporate structure that greets her at the door with a multitude of disappointments because of her skin color. And I couldn't take another woman of color being aged out because she is slightly on the older side; she too has worked too hard to lean out now.

The Good News

Over my career I received rave annual reviews, but I didn't use those opportunities to discuss advancement or give detailed accounts of projects that helped my company's bottom line. It was much later in my career when I started to look at every move as a strategic opportunity, which led me to understand my worth. I noticed that some of my counterparts excelled at this and rose up the ladder. The good news is I finally got it right. It took work, but over time I became the curator of my career. I became the architect strategically building my career one brick at a time. I was promoted, negotiated a six-figure salary, and even negotiated my way to working from home. And not only that, I still had opportunities to advance while working outside the office. I am not an expert, but I know a thing or three about upward mobility. I wrote *The Memo* so you could feel seen, gain insider workplace hacks, and secure your seat at a table that makes sense for you. Anybody who wants the sauce should have access to the sauce! And that, my friends, is why I felt compelled to share the recipe with you.

Let me give you just a little background on why this book matters so much to me. Three years ago I started a business called The Memo LLC, a career development platform for women of color, with my cofounder Lauren Broussard. We help women of color prepare for their seat at the table by providing resources, curricula, and community. At our career boot camps, I shared tips on how to successfully navigate the workplace. I felt it was time to share with a larger audience—the ones who have been leaning in and felt left out. What about the women of color who didn't get *The Memo*? The Memo is the how-to guide I wish I'd had when I entered the workforce. It could have served as the career coach that I could afford! If I had known the ugly truths, I would have shed fewer tears. Most importantly, I would have stood up and advocated for myself in a way that made my superiors and colleagues take notice. I would have had the confidence to establish boundaries in a toxic work environment, and possibly advanced faster because I would have recognized my value much earlier. It's hard navigating the workplace and trying to figure out whether your colleagues want you at their table. I believe it's important to acknowledge these systems that are in place to hold us back, yet now is the time to call them out and make it rain glass ceilings. Ladies, we have a lot of catching up to do, so let's get in FORMATION and Secure Those Seats!

Your Assignment

When things get tough at work, view me as your career coach, rooting for you every step of the way. When you feel like you want to lean out, pick up *The Memo* and find your fuel to get you to your end goal. Listen, I've hit some of the same obstacles that you have experienced or might experience—we've probably even shed the same tears over the same unfair work sh—! But you know what, the stories that you will find in this book come from women who look like you and whom you can use as mentors when you feel isolated. We are in this together! There is no white person on the planet who will know what it's like to be young or old, melanated, and gifted, so make sure you own it! But before I get too Tony Robbins on you, I forgot one thing: the Haters and the Skeptics. There will be people who read this book and say, "They better take me the way I am" and "Who gon' check me, boo?" This book might not be for you. There is a game to get ahead, and if you want to play, I can help you win! Once we get our seats, we then have the ability to change the way the game is set up, and that should ultimately be our goal.

In the meantime, I want *The Memo* to serve as a resource for recent college graduates who want to put their best foot forward, for the women feeling stuck and not sure where or what to do in their career. This book is for you. For the person that hasn't found a mentor or a sponsor, this book is for you. For the woman who is experiencing ageism and wants a new fresh perspective on how to move forward, despite bias! And wouldn't it be great if white men and women picked up *The Memo* to gain insight on how to be a better advocate, manager, or leader in the workplace? *The Memo* does not discriminate! It's everything I wish someone would have written and sent out to me!

2

BUILDING YOUR SQUAD

ONE CRITICAL PART of my success, outside of God parting the Red Sea so Moses could "let my people go," is building a killer squad (network). There is a prophet known as Sean "Diddy" Combs. He says, in the song "Big Poppa" by Notorious B.I.G., "Tell your friends to get with my friends, and we can be friends." This is how relationships work! When we build great squads, in turn, people want to introduce us to their squads. This is what some in the business world call "social capital." The right social capital is better than any glass of sweet tea on a hot summer's day. I could write an entire book on how building great relationships with people opened the door to meeting other amazing people, which allowed me to introduce them to other amazing people. But in this chapter, I want to talk about different ways to build your squad inside and outside the workplace.

Some of you more seasoned millennials might remember Myspace and the Top 8. I don't know if Tom Anderson realized it, but he was setting us up to build out our future networks. Your Top 8 comprised your ride-or-die friends. It actually caused a lot of drama because, out of all your friends, you had to choose eight of your most important squad members. Fast forward; we now have LinkedIn to help us manage our networks in a more adult way, yet I still believe it's important for us to think in terms of our business Top 8. Who are those business contacts we need to help us advance in our careers? If you can't think of eight people off the top of your head, then what in the heck are you doing with your life? Okay, maybe that was a little harsh, but I want you to start building today!

Let me break this all the way down to the lowest common denominator and show you the importance of a strong network before we move on. Oprah crushed it, and then we met Gayle King, we met Iyanla Vanzant, we met Dr. Phil, and then Dr. Oz. Who are those people in your squad? Now I understand we all can't have what Oprah has, but we can have our version. My alter ego is called the "Seat Creator." I like to create seats for other women. When I think about these positions, I envision myself being Oprah: I am pulling my squad together. We support, encourage, and push each other toward greatness. Do you have people in your life like this? In the age of the Internet, we have the power and access to create our dream Top 8.

I know y'all love a good example, so check this out. I was a guest on a podcast called *Trailblazers*. This is a favorite podcast for black professionals, hosted by Stephen A. Hart (no relation). I was in episode 60. How did I become a guest on this podcast? A man named Shawn Dove, the CEO of Campaign for Black Male Achievement, introduced me to Stephen. How did I meet Shawn? A man named Allan Ludgate from Deloitte introduced me to Shawn. How did I meet Allan? I approached Allan at a networking event and started to build a relationship with him. Eventually, Allan felt comfortable opening up his network to me (see the way social capital works?). Now here is the kicker. After being a guest on the podcast, I realized that one of my mentors in my head, Miko Branch, cofounder of the natural hair care business Miss Jessie's, was a guest in a previous episode. Miko is an entrepreneur of color and one I have followed and admired for years. My company was planning our first Women of Resilience Awards to celebrate women of color in business. I asked Stephen if he would introduce me to Miko. Long story short: eventually Stephen made the intro, and we honored Miko at our event. None of this would have happened without a network. We need one inside the office, and we need one outside. And it's important to note that relationship building is reciprocal. I don't just get what I need; I make sure to help my network get what they need too. That is why I like to create more seats at any table I sit at. Who are you inviting to your table?

Now that example might be way too much for you and scare you away from networking as a whole, but I want you to know that you have the ability to create your dream squad. As you read this chapter, start to think of your squad in terms of two teams. One squad is your internal network (at work) and the second squad is your external network (outside work). Personally, I believe you need communities of people working on your behalf on both sides of your life! We will start with building your squad at work, because you spend the most time there, and then work our way into steps to help you meet others to add to your external squad.

After 6

An important aspect of building your squad at work is putting yourself out there. And there are plenty of books about how to create a network, but what most won't tell you is one simple but important factor: stuff happens after 6 p.m. Minda, what you do mean, stuff happens after 6 p.m.? Well . . . I'm glad you asked. Not every business decision occurs between the hours of 8 a.m. and 5 p.m. After running career boot camps for almost three years, I've heard countless women of color say, "I don't want to go to happy hour with my colleagues." My response is virtually always the same. You don't have to go to happy hour, but you know who is at happy hour? Becky. Becky is going to be at happy hour, having a great time, laughing at all of Bob's jokes, and finding out the tea, while you're at home watching old episodes of *Girlfriends* on BET, wondering how Becky got promoted. We have to put ourselves out there so our colleagues get to know us. Now, I am not saying promotions only happen this way, but now Bob feels more comfortable with Becky. He sees that she has an excellent personality, she is a team player, and she wants more. Becky put in more effort to position herself for the win the next time a promotion comes up. The irony is Becky might not even be qualified for that promotion, but she was in the right place at the right time. The happy hours, the BBQs, the birthday parties, this is where employees find out what's coming down the pipeline. These are opportunities to shine outside the workplace, opportunities for you to learn more about the decision-makers and for them to observe you away from work. There's a lot to learn about Bob, and you won't always get the opportunity to fraternize at work; in order to find out, you have to get out of your cube and be seen at the places where Bob is doling out his intimate information, like the fact that he has five kids or what his favorite cake flavor is. If women of color don't participate in after-work activities, then we will miss out.

Let me make it just a little clearer. Do you know why Becky brought in red velvet cupcakes for Bob's birthday? Because she found out he loves red velvet cupcakes at the last team dinner you didn't attend. HELLO, knock, knock, McFly, do you see a pattern here? Are women of color all over the country going to let the Beckys outshine them because they were too tired after work or because they didn't think it took all that? Perhaps if more women of color shared a few laughs with Bob, they might have found out about this position that needed to be filled and positioned themselves for it, and then Bob might have been more prone to consider them for the role over Becky. But Becky knew how to play the game. The internal networking game has to be played if you want to get ahead.

Again, I'm not saying that birthday parties and weekends in the Hamptons advance careers, but they sure won't hurt, and it shows your colleagues another side of you. In my years in corporate America, I have found that white people want to feel like they know you. They want to feel like your "friends." As black and brown women, we just want to do our job, do it well, and get the hell out of Dodge. And if women of color don't act like we want to be "friends" in the workplace, then tons of assumptions are made about us—fill in the stereotype here. We are constantly fighting those lovely labels some of our colleagues like to adorn us with, so it's important to take every opportunity to kill those harmful stereotypes that tend to follow us from workplace to workplace. They can't say that we are aggressive or hard to communicate with if they experience us in different environments where we relax a little. And sometimes that requires going out of our way to attend after-work activities with our colleagues.

One of our most popular career boot camps at The Memo is How to Leverage Your Network, and the common thread among the women in The Memo community is that networking inside one's company can be hard. It's true—it can be. But building relationships internally is just as important as building them externally. The whole idea of "playing the game" comes into play at the office. And as much as I hate advising our members on how to play it, moving up requires being a team player to some degree. Becky isn't the only fun one; women of color can be fun too! But when will the powers that be have the opportunity to see this side of us if we never engage outside the workplace?

Years ago, I worked for a manager who liked his team to go out to lunch when it was a colleague's birthday. The expectation was that everyone would make time during their lunch break to celebrate as a group. Some of my colleagues wouldn't go, because they felt they shouldn't be obligated to celebrate someone else's birthday on their lunch break. Nine times out of ten, I would attend these birthday lunches, because (1) it signaled to my colleagues that I appreciated them, even if I didn't; (2) my manager asked each of us to go, so clearly it was important to him; and (3) my attendance allowed me to

learn the dynamics of our team and hear some of the office gossip that I would never have known otherwise. I don't like office gossip, but it taught me whom I needed to connect with and whom I probably should stay clear of at work. I was also able to observe my colleagues in another light and learn who I could trust to add to my squad. As you consider adding your colleagues to your Top 8, it's important you know who is for you and who is against you. Not everyone at work is your friend, and when you're not in the room, who can you trust to advocate on your behalf if the situation calls for advocacy? In addition, who do you think is worth your advocacy? Just as you're using out-of-work chances to show others who you are, you're also learning who they are. You won't see your colleagues' true colors sitting in your cube or passing each other on the way to get coffee in the break room. You need to see what they are like on the outside—up close and personal. Lastly, during these team lunches, I became closer with my manager. My manager was silly, unfiltered, yet intellectual. I tended to be more buttoned up and not so playful—more on the serious side. These lunches allowed him to see a more playful side of me, and that allowed him to become more comfortable with me. Even though I was one of the top performers on his team, me laughing at his jokes seemed to be what impressed him the most. Go figure! As you can see, going out with your colleagues might not be the most convenient and comfortable thing to do, but try it out. It will take time to ramp up your network, but start now and in the words of New Kids on the Block, "Step by step, ooh, baby!"

Let's take a look at how this worked for another Memo woman. I spoke with one of our members, Yolanda, and she

recalls never wanting to play the game. She hated when the Beckys played it; she hated seeing fellow people of color schmooze just to get invited to lunch with the Bobs of the workplace. She mentioned that when she entered the workforce she vowed to never become one of "those people" because it seemed fake. Yolanda chose not to play the game within her organization, and over time her colleagues started to perceive her as what *Basketball Wives* star Evelyn Lozada called "A non muthaf—in' factor!" They stopped inviting her to the group lunches and only engaged her when they needed too. Yolanda started to notice that her colleagues had opportunities that she didn't. Perhaps if she had taken the time to get to know them, she might have found an internal champion. Yolanda said, "I wish someone would have pulled me to the side and showed me that making the decision not to engage with my colleagues would hurt my chances to advance. I was already the only person of color in the office. I leaned out and that hurt me." I understand that every woman of color might not feel comfortable golfing with Bob and the boys, but attending something outside the office now and then is a good first step. So don't be afraid to go out to lunch with work homies once a month, or if everyone is dressing up for the office Halloween party, find some orange to put on, grab some candy at the Dollar Store, set up a bowl of candy at your desk, and have a little fun!

Be Strategic

Every good thing happens with strategy. So networking events outside work with your colleagues are not, I repeat, they are not, opportunities to get drunk and turnt up. They are op-

Building Your Squad

portunities to advocate for yourself. I remember when I was working twelve-hour days, and some of my colleagues and senior leaders would ask me to go out after work. Let's keep it real, it's been a long day, and I have seen my colleagues all week. I want to go home and catch up on my episodes of *Insecure*. But I knew the people who already sat at the table would be there, and this would be an excellent opportunity to have some face time. I am all for the face time. Being in an industry in which I traveled almost every week, I would sometimes go to cities and stay in the same hotel with my colleagues. I hated this type of group travel because it meant I would have to "hang out" after a long day. I had spent all day and night with them, and now they expected me to give up the few hours of downtime I had left.

Yet I must admit—as we've discussed—these were some of the best opportunities for me to get to know my colleagues (for better or worse) and, most importantly, for them to see a different side of me. The Minda who wasn't so formal. The Minda who could take a joke and throw one right back. I learned so much. I used these times to make small talk with our senior leaders and casually discuss my plans to advance within the company. Not in an obnoxious way, but being authentic and intentional. Sometimes we have to push ourselves if we want to rise up the ladder.

If advancing is not important to you, then go back to your hotel room and flip through those five channels that consist of three Fox News stations. And remember, if everyone goes out for happy hour, you might consider going too and ordering a Shirley Temple; you just need to be seen for ten to fifteen minutes, then break out! The point is—use this as an opportunity

27

to find out how your colleagues perceive and engage with you and find ways to engage with them!

Relationship Building with Management

It is not the powers that be that need to get to know their employees, but us employees who have to position ourselves so the powers that be get to know us! Just like you, I had to learn how to network and build my squad. Building relationships with your colleagues might be a piece of cake for you, but how do you network up? It took someone pulling me to the side and giving me some pointers. And it's my duty to pass them along to you. Even Jesus said, "No branch can bear fruit by itself; it must remain on the vine!" And who knows more about networking than Jesus? A wise mentor of mine told me, "Make rounds." I laugh about it now, but it was one of the best pieces of advice I have received. I was located on the same floor as the most senior person in our division. Of course, he was in an office, and I was in a cube (window view, I might add). If our fearless leader wasn't traveling, he was taking meetings in his office. It was not uncommon for us to go weeks without seeing each other. And even if we had seen each other, I am not sure if he was ever checking for me. So, if I knew he would be in the office or had a standing appointment with someone else, I would "make rounds." I would strategically plot when his standing appointment would leave his office and the door would be open, and I would slide by and say hello. This, folks, is face time. I would do this a couple of times a month if we were both in the office. Each time, the conversations got lengthier, and when the time was right, I asked if I could schedule an appointment to talk with him about some ideas I had. He welcomed it and from that day forward, he thought of me for committees, opportunities, and advancement; he created a seat at the table for me. But I had to put in the work. It took over six months before anything came out of these brief hallway chats. And as I was doing this, I didn't know if anything would ever come of it. And I also knew that "Rob" might never have stopped by my cube for face time with me. Why would he? This is just one of many examples of building strategic relationships with your leadership. Get creative in how you do it (but not too creative, no showing up at their house uninvited!). Attending all the happy hours and birthday parties isn't just because—everything should be done with strategy and with the purpose of positioning you closer to your goals. You gotta come through dripping (Cardi B voice)!

Mentor Versus Sponsor

Now that we're thinking about face time with management and how to network up, we should get clear on how to establish that support system with those higher up the ranks than you. There has been a lot of debate about the definition of mentors versus sponsors and the roles they play in access to upward mobility at work. A mentor is someone whom you trust to give you advice on certain life or career matters. For example, I met with my mentor to discuss how to get Rob's attention and stand out. She provided me with guidance on how to have meaningful interactions with him. We brainstormed scenarios, and she left it up to me to figure out what route I felt comfortable taking. I am sure you can already think of people in your life that provide you similar guidance. Although we never had any formal conversations about her being my mentor, our relationship just naturally progressed into mentor/mentee. Let's say that my mentor worked in human resources and during the next senior staff meeting, when they go over open positions, she recommends my name to Rob as a potential candidate. Now I am on Rob's radar, and I get an opportunity to interview for this position. She is now serving as my sponsor. She put herself out there to amplify my work. You might consider finding one of each. Either way you slice it, you need both as you ascend to the top of the food chain.

And one last thing about sponsorship. I didn't ask her to sponsor me. This is something someone will typically do on their own, to show you how invested they are in your success. In many cases, finding a mentor is a lot easier; that is something you could ask of someone, and most of the time, people love giving out advice so mentorship is not as daunting. Sponsorship, on the other hand—that takes some true relationship building. Most people, even those in positions of power, are not going to stick their necks out for someone they don't know. Now in a perfect workplace, your direct manager would serve as your sponsor. That person should know your career goals and plans and provide opportunities for growth, but we know most managers aren't always invested in the success of the people they manage (that is another book to write).

So what do you look for in mentors and sponsors? Unfortunately, in corporate America or the not-for-profit world, many women of color don't have mentors and sponsors who look like them. In other words, most of the people in positions of power are not of color, and we are expected to once again fit ourselves into a one-size-fits-all model for career development. Don't get me wrong, good advice is good advice and a leg up is a leg up, but it would be nice if women of color didn't always have to look outside their workplace to find champions they can relate to. During my career, I've had various mentors. I formally solidified a mentor/mentee relationship with some and had an unwritten partnership (like the one described above) with others. My mentors are men and women, different races and ages—that diversity is a benefit for me. I might go to one of my mentors for salary negotiation advice, and I might go to another on how to gain buy-in from my colleagues or how to dress to impress. Everyone serves a purpose! They aren't all necessarily people I speak to every day or even people who will stay mentors forever, but they are people I trust to have my best interests at heart.

Still not convinced you need to cultivate mentors and sponsors, and how they're different? Another example: later, Rob became my sponsor too. He had the power and ability to place me on committees and promote me when the time was right, and he had the authority to help me increase my salary. Because he trusted what I brought to the table, he could vouch for me. Sometimes your mentor and sponsor can be the same person, and other times he or she serves specific roles. I encourage the women who come to our networking boot camps to identify and secure a mentor and a sponsor as part of their winning squad. I couldn't have moved forward without Rob's buy-in. Maybe, just maybe, I could have "worked" my way to the top, but I strongly believe you need a few people at the table who will usher you in, and that takes building out that relationship. When I look back on all the people I have worked

31

with over the years, many of the ones who "made it" had some-one who pulled them up with them.

Another thought: I hope you will find ways to mentor and sponsor other people as well. For example, I had a speaking en-gagement that I had to cancel due to some health issues. When I reached out to the coordinators, I explained the situation and offered up the names of women I thought would be phenom-enal replacements. Oddly enough, I didn't really know them, but I had shared the stage with them before and recognized their talent. I used my influence to elevate them. I could vouch for their talents. One of them was called upon, and the rest is history. Now one of the women I suggested didn't have a so-cial media presence, and some places can be funny when their speakers don't have an online presence. They took my word and used her. They ended up booking her again! I sponsored her. She didn't ask me; I did it on my own. Success rarely ever hap-pens alone. And as I said before, success is not a solo sport.

Peers

Lastly, not all of your squad need to be upper management. Your peers can be mentors as well. Peer mentorship is an awe-some relationship-building experience with your colleagues. You can bounce ideas off each other, and oftentimes this will lead to building a squad of workplace friends. Your colleagues can serve as great advocates as well. Do you have a work-wife or work-husband? I am a firm believer that we should build relationships with principal individuals that make hiring deci-sions and those who can help along the way, but don't discount the people that work alongside you or in other departments.

You should make it a priority to build relationships with your colleagues who will have your back from day to day and want to see you win. The people you can run to when keeping it real goes wrong (Hi, Dave Chappelle) or you just can't deal with Becky that day. Having a sounding board with people on the inside who are trustworthy goes a long way! I was going through a tough time at one point in my career (I will talk about this situation in Chapter 4) with another colleague; if it hadn't been for my work-wife, I don't know how I would have survived the torture. She helped me stay sane, and I knew someone had my back. It makes a difference if you are the only person of color in your office; your work-spouse can help you feel less secluded. In other words, we all need advocates helping us advance. And again, this is where reciprocity takes place. You get to be this for another colleague as well. When I assemble my work crew, I typically like to make work friends with someone in IT support and human resources and, of course, my peers that I work with every day. Start to think of who you want on your squad!

Keep the Relationship Going

Relationship building is an art form, and following up is what makes networking—work! But how do we make time to maintain these new and existing relationships? First, we have to overcome what I call the busyness factor. I cringe every time I say the word *busy*; I cringe when I hear someone else tell me how *busy* they are. Busy must be the most overused word in the dictionary at this point. Is your ego so big that you think no one else is busy? Guess what? Everyone is busy! I am laughing out loud thinking there used to be a day when I sat on the phone and would talk to my friends or family for hours. Now I can barely stand being on the phone for more than ten minutes. Not because I don't want to talk to them; it's because of the busyness factor. I don't have time to sit on the phone most days for more than thirty minutes at a time. But with that said, I know that to keep up with relationships I value, I must implement meaningful ways to stay in touch. A few that have worked well for me:

1. I use a journal or calendar notifications to remind me it's time to follow up. Because of all that's going on, you might not remember that Bob's daughter Bonnie is graduating from college and you need to send her a card.

2. At least once a quarter, I try to connect with the people that I consider to be in my Top 8. I value their input and care about what's going on in their lives, so they are always top of mind for me. That means at least four times a year they should hear from me.

3. I am a super old skool kind of girl, and I buy a dope box of assorted greeting cards and some stamps and keep them in my bag. This allows me to drop folks a card when I think about them or, if I had an amazing meeting with someone, to send them a card in the mail right before they forget about me (instead of sending them a generic email that might get lost in the shuffle).

Each of these helps me to stay in touch, and they don't require a lot on my part because I got stuff to do too. I don't like it when I hear from people only when they want something from me. It's nice to get a "Hey, just checking in. . . . " I like to know how folks are doing too. There are people in my life I haven't physically seen in years, but I let them know what's going on with me, and because they still feel invested in me, when I need something they do it because they know I am not just using them! We have a real relationship that I took time to cultivate.

No matter how busy I am, I must keep those relationships going. It doesn't mean I need to call them every week and talk for three hours. It means I can't afford to go for extended periods of time without connecting with them. I think the follow-up is the most important ingredient in the recipe for sustaining your network. God blessed Michaela Cole with the power to write a genius show like *Chewing Gum*, he blessed Gabrielle Union with phenomenal skin that would put most twenty-year-olds to shame, and he blessed me with being a good networker. I didn't initially look at this as a thing to brag about. I didn't go around telling people I was the best networker in the game. What I did value is that I was a good people person and I cultivated healthy relationships. I am always humbled by the people I meet who allow me to get to know them. Now I see this trait as a gift from God. In the words of Jay-Z, "Whatever God give me, I'm cool." And for the record, following up doesn't always mean meeting people face-to-face. It could be a text when their child graduates from college. It could be a holiday card every December. Or something like a voice memo just catching them up. If you don't foster the network you have created, it will fail. The people in your life don't want to feel like you're using them because they only hear from you when you need something. None of us likes dealing with people like that, so don't be one of those people! I keep in touch with people that I met on my first job. I have spent holidays with former clients who have become friends. It takes work to stay in touch, but I believe real relationships will require that of you. Easy ones slip away. Please don't let busy get in your way. And if you think of another word to use, share it with me!

I'll Show You How to Network

Let's talk about networking. I know some of you are probably cringing at the very thought of having to go to a networking event or a holiday party. Networking and relationship building should be skills in your tool kit. If your network is on the weaker side, what steps will you take to strengthen it? If it's strong, what will you do to enhance it? For the ones who say "I am not a people person" or "I am an introvert," I realize being shy and not wanting to put yourself out there is a thing. There are days I have to push myself to go to networking events and approach people like Allan. I think back to my childhood and remember *Jem and the Holograms*. Jerrica adopts this persona called Jem with the help of a holographic computer named Synergy. The holograms the computer projects onto her help her pull off being truly outrageous. Get you a Synergy and stop playing! Get out of your own way. Women of color can no longer afford to hold onto the tagline "I am not this type of person or that kind of person." Do you remember the 2006 movie *Something New* with Sanaa Lathan and Simon Baker? Sanaa's character Kenya Moore had all of these "things" she didn't do, like dogs, hiking, and colors. She chalked it up to being a little anal, but also to black women not doing certain things. Eventually, she allowed herself to step out of her comfort zone and live her best life! So you don't have to be NeNe Leaks and be the life of the party, but you could be like Charlotte from *Sex in the City*, not as outgoing but someone who would still put herself out there and mingle.

It's going to be extremely hard to have a seat at the table if you are not a people person. And sitting at a table alone gets lonely. I was working on a short project in Austin, Texas. I didn't know anyone in Austin or the surrounding area other than my colleagues who were also sent to work on this project, and we didn't know each other all that well. I was a young and vibrant woman at the time, and I got tired of spending my Friday and Saturday nights alone in my hotel or temporary apartment. I had to push myself to get out and meet people. This meant I had to go to movies and restaurants alone. Now, I felt weird at first, but I knew I had to put myself out there. So I would go out to restaurants that I had heard about and sit at the bar. Eventually, someone else who was alone would sit at the bar and next thing you know, I made a friend. Now, we might not have exchanged numbers after our meals, but it helped me get out of my comfort zone. In addition, I started to create a relationship with one of my coworkers by inviting her out for dinner. She was also in Austin "alone," and we got to build our relationship. We worked on the project together for only a few months, but I still have that relationship today. I don't think I've seen her since 2006, but we have always stayed connected. And one of those people I met sitting at the bar in Austin on a random Wednesday night, I met up with again about ten years later in Los Angeles. You will never know if you don't put yourself out there.

Now going out alone or initiating dinners with colleagues might be too hard for some of you to just run out and do tonight. I get it! But something you might consider doing is going out to networking events in your industry or an industry that intrigues you and taking one of your friends with you. That creates a little less pressure than if you show up alone. Make it a fun game with one of your friends. You each have to talk to someone new or exchange business information with at least three people. This will force you to work the room, not just stand and sip cocktails with your friend all night. Many of the people I meet at networking functions keep in touch with me on LinkedIn or other social media platforms. Social media makes life a little easier. I don't have to give out my number to strangers. The last thing I will say about network-ing is this: I try to go to a networking event at least a couple of times a month. I find them online and show up. Often I go alone because all my friends are "busy." I have learned over the years that I am my best advocate, and I consider myself a go-getter. I go get what I want and bring it back! I don't believe we should get comfortable and put a cap on our net-work. Industries are steadily changing, and you never know who might be able to help you down the road or whom you might be able to help.

You Can Do It

The cool thing about building your network is that you have the power to figure out who you want in your Top 8. If you don't have a strong network, think through who you want to have as part of your squad and go out and meet those people. Use professional organizations or conferences to help you get in the rooms with the people you want to meet. The network that I have built has required me to do the work to build it. And one more thing . . . I wish that some people of color would stop saying "I didn't go to an Ivy League school" and all this other crap. Neither did I. Sitting around blaming your work situation on your pedigree or lack of access doesn't get you any further along in this game. So what, Katie and Megan went to Princeton and now have this incredible network to tap into to help them land a new job. Life is unfair! My dream would have been to have a Stanford network when I graduated from college, but those weren't the cards I was dealt. My cards were a year of junior college and a lot of student loans. So I created a "Stanford" network on my own.

Building my own squad allowed me to sit in the living room of the great author, Toni Morrison, in upstate New York. Creating my own network positioned me to sit across the table from one of the most well-known venture capitalists in the country, Ben Horowitz. And if that isn't enough proof for you, it allowed my first press article about The Memo LLC to be featured in *Essence* magazine. It took putting myself out there and advocating for myself, even when I felt like no one else was advocating for me.

So, you ask, how did the article in *Essence* happen? I met a woman at a networking event (I went alone), and we sat next to each other. We chatted for maybe fifteen to twenty minutes about what we do, and I told her about my business. She never said who she worked for! A few months later she reached out to me and asked me to contribute to this article she was working on for *Essence* magazine. Look at God! I didn't have to beg or have a million social media followers for that to happen. I went to this networking event with no motive but to meet other people. As women of color, we hold the power to create! No matter what hand you're being dealt, the people who win, win because they played a winning hand. As I said before, it's damn near impossible to re-create Oprah's success, but it is possible to figure out what your Top 8 should look like. Think through the next few months and start building out your internal and external networks. Think through who might make a good mentor and who you might be able to establish a relationship with that might one day become your sponsor. And don't forget that relationship building happens on both sides. Don't be a leech! Start creating, maintaining, and building today. Make Oprah proud!

3

THE POLITICS

I F YOU'VE BEEN working for any amount of time by now, you probably understand there are unwritten and written rules for getting a seat at the table. Cue the music, please: "Well, I'm not gon' cry, I'm not gon' shed no tears." Office politics. Whew. Lawd. Jesus. It's a thing. It's a thing. Navigating office politics is like trying to save the princess from King Koopa in the original Mario Bros. Women of color have to go through a lot of fireballs and some spare lives before getting to our seats. And even if we manage to make it to the final level, we might not receive a party or a promotion. Many of us haven't been privy to the cheat codes that help us to skip a level or two. And college didn't teach a class on navigating office politics, although it should have been mandatory. I was under the assumption that every hard-working employee would have equal opportunity to advance; little did I know this whole meritocracy thing was a sham. I had to do my job in addition to jumping through so many hoops, kissing a lot of babies, and performing at a level that would make me stand out, but some of my white colleagues could do the bare minimum and reap the benefits. There were points in my career when I questioned if a seat at the table was even worth the fight, yet I knew I had to keep going so there would be representation around the tables where I took my place. My hope was that the next woman of color to join me wouldn't have to navigate unnecessary waters. It took me a while to figure out the rules and align myself with the right workplace alliances, but once I did, I knew I had to share the sauce. Now, all working environments are not the same, but every office has its politics. And knowing how to finesse the office politics will make or break your career. It's crucial women of color understand how to overcome a rigged system so we can create seats. My great-grandmother used to say, "We are God's soldiers marching in the army." She ain't never lied! I spent an entire year in one department that felt like a battlefield every day. As a black woman I've had plenty of what I call Rachel Maddow moments, when "I have to talk myself off the ledge." Those moments at work when I knew darn well I wouldn't have to experience this nonsense if my skin were a different color.

Office politics are systematically ruthless. Office politics enable 45 to hire all his family members for positions they are not qualified for. Office politics explain how someone like Jefferson "racist" Sessions could end up as our country's attorney general even the late Mrs. Coretta Scott King warned us of his ways. Office politics will have you fired from your job because you spoke out against someone in power. Oh, and please let us not forget, these same politics will have Republicans trying to push a black man and a white man who both have a history of negative behavior toward women onto the Supreme Court. Office politics can be brutal, unfair, and often an "old boys club" that many women of color don't receive an invitation to join. I have even seen some colleagues forced into early retirement because a new person in power did not like them. As women of color, we must acknowledge that these systems exist and figure out whose team we need to be on to help move us forward in our careers. Or at least whom we need to be civil toward so we don't lose our status in the workplace. The thing is . . . office politics is some sh— and how we navigate them will be critical to our workplace success.

The Bias

Before we dive too deep into navigating office politics, I think we should first address conscious and unconscious bias. I believe these conjoined twins set the stage for how office politics erode the workplace, leaving a lot of talented and tenured people overlooked and undervalued—more than likely people of color. I often hear white people say that unconscious bias doesn't exist. That's like saying the White Walkers don't exist on *Game of Thrones*: all well and good unless they're coming after you. Typically, unconscious and sometimes conscious bias are directed toward underrepresented groups in the workplace. I find it funny that often the most represented group in the workplace dictates the existence of bias. White people shouldn't get the privilege of whiteness and the pleasure of setting the definition of bias. Janet Jackson had a song called *The Pleasure Principle*, but I don't think that is what she meant!

It's almost like watching the nightly news and the panelists are discussing racism in America and no people of color are represented on the panel. Really? Privilege is a helluva drug!

Let's break down bias. Bias, by definition, is prejudice against or in favor. And to be fair, each of us has participated in bias at some point in time. It is not reserved for white folks only! Workplace bias can rear its ugly head in various arenas: hiring, promotion, and job duties, just to name a few. One woman told me that she had been working in her position for a couple of years when the executive director left the company. Jonelle then became the interim ED and held that title for over a year while they interviewed candidates. It never dawned on the committee of white men and women that Jonelle (a black woman) was the best person for the job until one of their donors asked, Why are you looking to fill the position when you already have the most qualified woman doing the job? Shortly afterward, the hiring committee gave Jonelle the position permanently. Do you see how workplace politics directly affected whether or not Jonelle got a promotion and a new title? Just because Jonelle didn't have the "credentials" the committee thought an ED should have, they counted her out—even though she had been doing the job for two years. Stories like Jonelle's happen each and every day to women of color.

Another example of bias in the hiring process is all the problems people had with my first name. My government name is Yassminda. As beautiful as I think my name is, I had to start using Minda at a young age because my teachers had a hard time pronouncing it. I remember being five years old and frustrated with adults; I guess the "Y" prevented them from even trying. In kindergarten I told my family to start calling me Minda, and from that day forward Yassminda became invisible. During my freshman year in college, my professors struggled with pronouncing my name or remained silent, staring at their sheet of paper, and I would automatically yell out, "It's Yassminda, but you can call me Minda." When I entered the workforce, I chose not to use Yassminda on my résumé because of what I now realize to be an awareness and avoidance of bias. Back then, I had no idea what the hell bias was, but I had enough life experience to know that my full name made some white people uncomfortable. I consciously knew that Minda would make white people feel more comfortable because it's almost like Linda. I felt Yassminda was too ethnic and would hurt my chances of being considered for the first round of interviews. That was a decision that I shouldn't have had to make to appease white people, yet people of color learn to appease white people at a young age.

Making the decision to shorten my government name might have solved a temporary problem in an all-white workplace by getting me in the door, but at whose expense? I denied myself the use of my given name to appease a group of people who wouldn't take the time to learn to pronounce it. I didn't realize how damaging this was to me in my formative years, but now I look back on my decision in two ways. On one level, it was a simple choice: Minda was less threatening, and in the industry I worked in, with many wealthy individuals, my name was often the first thing popping into their inbox. I knew that Minda would go over more smoothly. But eventually, I got so used to using Minda that when someone did call me Yassminda it felt foreign. On another level, I am mad at myself for feeding into the bullsh— of perpetuating the vicious cycle of making white people feel comfortable with me being black at work. The water cooler talk among women of color is being able to bring one's full self to work, yet I can't even go by my own freaking name. My ancestors were brought to America with their African names, and after being sold into slavery they received "easier" names like Harriet, Sally, and Belle, a.k.a. white names! I guess this oppression made its way into the workplace. Makes me wonder if the former secretary of state Condoleezza Rice battled over using Condoleezza or Leezza.

For the record, there are consequences on both sides. If you choose to go the route I did, make sure you understand the consequences it could have for you on the inside. I might've been considered for more interviews by choosing to use Minda over Yassminda, but over time I hated that I had to even make that choice. And once I started to make small compromises on my name, it was easier to change my hairstyle to something that white people find more palatable when dealing with people of color. Another term for this is "respectability politics," coined by author and professor Evelyn Brooks Higginbotham. In American culture, respectability politics means, among other things, speaking a little more properly and making sure your hair is neat and "white looking." If you do these things, white people will treat you like one of them. And these politics are just another form of systemic racism reinforcing the idea that anything nonwhite is bad and unacceptable, so change your "colored" ways and "act white." That idea has been fed to one generation after another—I hope we stop encouraging it!

To play devil's advocate, what might my career have looked like if I had chosen to use Yassminda? I might have made some different choices that resulted in me being more concerned with my own comfort level. Perhaps I would have ended up in workplaces that honored my culture and my unique experience as an asset. I might not have gone on as many interviews, but I would have been able to use my given name. Maybe I missed out on that, or maybe I never would have reached the table like I did—but it stings on both sides. I don't have access to a DeLorean to go back to the future and fix it, though, and at the same time I don't regret it. And just remember, our names are the first thing we learn to write, so it's important we respect our own names. Think of it this way: do we want our children to experience the same frustration as we did? Future generations of women of color should understand at a young age the power we possess because as little girls, we don't have a lot of equity. Our names should mean everything to us!

If you're one of those women with a "hard" name, make everyone learn how to say it, if that's what you prefer being called. The conscious and unconscious bias inflicted on women of color in the workplace factor directly into some of the decisions women of color have to make on whether or not they will "play the game" with hopes of advancement or disrupt the rules and change the way the game is played! Unfortunately, something so simple like your name is part of how office politics work. If I read one more essay on "bringing your full self to work" by another white person, I think I might blow a gasket. It's easy for them to say that when they have spent hundreds of years telling us who we have to be to get ahead, and now some of us aren't sure what our authentic selves look like anymore! Our choice to show up authentically is exactly what has been discouraged by the "old boys club" that should have died a long time ago.

Let's take a look at a woman of color who chose a different route than mine, a friend of mine named Lady Tasha Jones. Lady Tasha and I were discussing her choice to keep her name when she entered the workforce, and she recounted her interactions with her white colleagues:

My parents never shortened my name, so I felt it was important not to do it either. When I entered the workforce, white people would state the following: Is that your real name? Is that the name on your birth certificate? Can I call you Tasha? What do you like to be called? I am going to give you a nickname! They just insisted on trying to call me everything but Lady Tasha.

Prior to making a career change, Lady Tasha worked in a predominantly black environment, and even though Lady Tasha isn't a common American name, her black and brown colleagues never questioned the authenticity of her name like her white colleagues. When Lady Tasha started her new job search, it was the first time she made the conscious decision to use Lady Jones on her résumé. She would no longer be working for an African American institution and thought she would have better chances of getting the interview by modifying her name. Lady Tasha told me she felt some kind of way about making the decision, and once hired, she immediately trained her new white colleagues to call her Lady Tasha. When they tried to give her a nickname, she called that sh— out!

Our counterparts Sally and Becky will never know what it's like to wake up in the morning and have to make the decision to bring their full black and brown glory to work or a modified version. They get the privilege of using Becky or Rebecca, and it won't dictate the jobs they can apply for or make hiring managers uncomfortable. As women of color we check all the boxes and play all the games, not for a promised corner office or increase in salary; we do everything for the sheer chance of getting ahead. Women of color have a lot of burdens to bear just rolling out of bed; our names and hair shouldn't be among them! And just for the record, we are still on some basic sh— like names; we haven't even got to hair yet! Some white hiring managers will call a Minda back before a Shaneka, even if Shaneka might be more qualified than Minda. White hiring managers already assume who Shaneka is before they meet her, and probably some black hiring managers, too.

These hiring biases correlate directly to many companies' use of blind-hiring practices to eliminate bias in their initial screenings. An example of blind hiring is removing the names of applicants from their résumés or job applications. Obviously, this doesn't solve all of the problems, but as you can see, bias can interrupt the process before a diverse candidate has the opportunity to interview. This is what some would call unconscious bias, making assumptions about the candidate without knowing it. If you are one of these hiring managers judging books before you see the cover, stop that!

To be candid, some of y'all are running around claiming unconscious bias like a badge of honor, when you know darn well it's conscious. There was this little thing that passed called the Civil Rights Act of 1964 that says an employer cannot discriminate based on race, color, religion, nationality, age, disability, or genetic information, yet many companies do the exact opposite and discriminate the hell out of people of color. And let's not forget the executive order signed by President John F. Kennedy in 1961 requiring government contractors to diversify their workforces. Why do you think we needed either if bias and discrimination were not taking place? It makes me sick to think the Trump administration would do anything to roll back these laws. If these laws are stripped away, people of color will have even less say in the workplace, and office politics/bias will be the law of the land. The jobs that many of my older relatives were able to apply for required them to serve at their table and we are not going back to those days!

Okay, let's get into it . . . hair! By now all the memos have gone out about women of color and their hair, yet there is still a national conversation. I was reading an article the other day about the Navy now allowing women of color to wear natural hairstyles. Wow, just wow! How many times must Solange tell you not to touch our hair? I was at a gala at Cipriani's in New York City and sat next to this white woman who was about thirty years older than me. We had an interesting conversation about workplace politics and exchanged pleasantries about our work. She recruits women to serve on corporate boards of directors. She kept telling me about this report Catalyst recently released regarding women and board seats. According to this report, women in the United States hold 27.8 percent of board seats at Fortune 500 Companies. I told her that women of color hold less than of 5 percent of those seats. She seemed confused when I continued to remind her that she shouldn't say "all women" when she really meant "white women." White people love to make sweeping generalizations about "women."

Long story short, after hours of candid conversation about race in the workplace, I flat out asked her, "If you have two women of color up for a board seat, and one of the women has her hair pulled back in a sleek ponytail, and the other has her hair in a natural hairdo (dreads or afro), which woman are you most comfortable with?" (Time out: When some white women think they have a newfound friend in a woman of color, they start saying a lot of politically incorrect sh—. I wanted to turn on some "Bodak Yellow" by Cardi B. and tell this woman, "Don't get comfortable!" Back to the story!) She said the woman with the ponytail, and that most boards would feel the same. She admitted this wasn't fair and blamed it on the culture of most companies. She went on to tell me that companies want to see clean-cut women of color. For the love of God, here we go again! So, you mean to tell me the woman wearing her hair in a natural style isn't clean-cut? I pressed her on this; my hope was she would stop and think about how stupid and weighted her decision-making process is on account of a woman's hair-style. That would mean many amazing natural-haired women are being overlooked because of their hair. If Keisha wears a weave with pink highlights, some view her as ghetto, but if Becky wears pink highlights, she's fun and cute. Stupid is as stupid does.

This woman must've forgotten she is a woman too and she is contributing to this backward way of thinking. She is the gatekeeper who allows white men to set the criteria! I think this is one of the main issues I have with many white women being accomplices instead of advocates. This woman could have chosen to use her influence for good; instead, she is help-ing the men she works with and continuing to perpetuate this idea that it's okay to police women. The event I attended took place shortly after the presidential election, and it was hard not to reflect on how many white men and women focused on Hillary Rodham Clinton's clothes and hair, and because of their choices, we are all living in the twilight zone. Men should not be setting the tone for what a woman does with any area of her life. Sigh. White women can't be trusted to always do the right thing on behalf of other women, especially women of color!

This is just one of many reasons women of color should be at the table. When more women of color sit at the table, an afro or dreads won't seem so scary.

During our career boot camps at The Memo, I hear many of our members talk about what it would be like to work for a company that doesn't care about superficial things like hair. And when our names won't be our plight and we can be un-apologetically black or brown. Almost sounds like heaven! It saddens me that I can't tell other women of color, "Hell yeah, girl, go to work the way you want and crush it!" Unfortunately, in the beginning, some of us can't show up at 9 a.m. unapolo-getically anything, without being met with opposition and ugly biases. My advice for women of color is to continue to knock it out the park when it comes to your performance at work, and then slowly show up in your full glory. With that said, don't forget that as women we can also decide not to work for companies or organizations that focus on blowouts over braids. We can and should make decisions that we can individually be comfortable with. I can't tell you what's right or wrong for you—maybe you can't stomach taking your time to show your full self at a company, or maybe you feel like you can change things from within. The choice will always be yours!

The GPS

Part of navigating office politics is knowing they do exist. And, I am not suggesting that white people don't also deal with office politics, but theirs isn't tied to race and gender. One of my former managers was a Jewish man. Jared had been at our organization for over a decade. I will always have a special place in my heart for Jared because he hired me for a position I wasn't qualified for on paper, but he knew I had the skills to be one of the best if I was just given the opportunity. He liked me and that was enough. That is one form of office politics. It's not always the most experienced or talented people who move ahead in their careers. Long before I was hired, Jared rubbed one of his former colleagues the wrong way, and she always felt some kind of way about him. They had some unknown beef that no one quite understood. She was promoted and became his boss. When she took her new position, like many executives newly overseeing a department, she led a reorganization. She had it out for Jared, and eventually he was forced into early retirement. Watching that experience go down was very eye-opening. If white people can be cut-throat to their own, you best believe they don't give a damn about me. She went on to force others out and replaced them with people she liked and those she considered friends. None were people of color. I learned so much about how power and politics will advance and shatter careers. Often, women of color don't have the opportunity to participate in these power moves, but we have been on the receiving end of the broken glass. When I look back, I wonder if Jared wished he hadn't burned that bridge with her earlier in their careers or wondered if he had kissed her ass, could he have found redemption? Who knows—office politics is a made-up game with fools' rules.

That said, here are a few lessons that I have learned about office politics that have served me well:

1. Don't burn bridges. Jared's situation is a textbook case of how not to treat people at work, because you never know when you might need them. From the janitor to the CEO, you don't know who you might need down the road, and it pays not to be a jerk. All I know is that boss lady held a grudge, and she had the sweetest revenge.

2. Don't be the office gossip. Spilling the office tea is not your part-time job. People will kiki with you all day about some good office gossip, but trust me, nobody respects the office gossip, nobody. For a long time I was scared to even share things with my colleagues because I didn't want anyone saying I said anything about anyone. I always kept my thoughts to myself because you just never know whom you can trust at work. Any colleague who easily gives up the tea on someone won't think twice about giving it up on you. So don't be that girl, and don't get caught up with that person either; if you value your reputation, you will stay clear of them. And if you are that person, well . . . um . . . moving right along.

3. Manage your behavior. Emotions run rampant in the office, and the key to navigating office politics is to manage your impulses. When you are interacting with colleagues with different backgrounds and personalities, from various departments, it's easy to want to take on a fight-or-flight mentality. American psychologist Walter Cannon coined the term "fight or flight." Essentially, an action triggers the release of hormones in your body that make you want to stay and fight over the situation or run away. And if you are a person of color at work, you have to learn very quickly to manage your impulses, or you would cuss somebody out seven out of the eight hours of the workday. I am not saying let people run over you, but what I am saying is, think first and then choose the best way to respond. There are so many battles that don't require you to react. You are a big girl. Learn how to regulate your emotions, or you're going to be reacting to every little thing, and if people see you as combative, that's no bueno for your career. It's politics as usual!

I want to spend a bit more time on managing your behavior, because I think this is where some women of color get labeled the "angry" this and the "feisty" that. I am a huge proponent of the motto, "It's not what you said; it's how you said it!" For a good part of my career, I let a lot of things slide when someone did me wrong at work or said something that might have been out of line. My easy button was to chalk it up to "They didn't mean any harm." After a while you start to realize that some of your colleagues do mean you harm. And I don't mean *Fright Night* harm, but they are only concerned with advancing their careers and not yours. After Hillary Clinton lost the 2016 presidential election, I would get so mad at white women. If a white woman said something dumb to me at work, I had to count backward to avoid saying something I would later regret. All the microaggressions, passive-aggressive comments, and racism had brought me to my breaking point. It was like a switch that was turned on, and I couldn't allow them to talk to me any kind of way anymore.

There was one colleague in particular I had a hard time trusting, yet I would still include her on projects because it was the right thing to do. Call me crazy—I am a sucker for collaboration. We had a decent working relationship and managed a few projects together, so we spoke frequently. She had worked with my manager at another company back in the day, so they were friends. But my manager knew I was one of her star employees and confided in me about various work-related matters. "Brenda" told my boss "Carla" over coffee that she didn't like how one of my direct reports handles things and that she should talk to me about it, because she was constantly having issues with him. She was questioning my management style. When I had my monthly meeting with Carla, she mentioned it to me in confidence so I could be aware of "Kyle's" behavior. I was so shocked that Brenda would tell my boss this when I talk to this heifer once a week. If she had a problem with someone on my team or how I manage them, then she could have talked to me directly about it. I voiced my concerns to Carla, and she told me that Kyle was having a tough time, being new on the job. Carla just wanted to make me aware of it. Now, if this had happened five to ten years ago, I would have sucked it up and kept moving. But I am too grown and too tired of the workplace BS to let it slide. Like the true professional I am, I told Carla that if she didn't mind, I would like to address this with Brenda. I felt like she stabbed me in the back by not giving me the common courtesy of talking to me first about Kyle's behavior. I would never go to her manager and do that to her. Carla had no problem with my plan because she knows I know how to handle my business. But I have to admit, I had to count to one hundred before I made that call to Brenda. I knew office politics could shape how I reacted to the information I heard if I handled this phone call the wrong way. I didn't want to ignore it because I work closely with her. And I knew that when I diplomatically addressed my concerns, she would know, I am not the one!

I called Brenda, and I wish I could have recorded that phone call. She backpedaled like a mofo. She said she thought she was talking to an old friend when she mentioned it in confidence and didn't realize it would be discussed with me. Well, well, well, girl, you got caught with your hands in the cookie jar and it's time for you to face the music. I told her that I was disappointed in her because we work together, and asked why, if she had an issue with Kyle, she didn't tell me about it instead of telling my boss. She had no good answer; she barely apologized because she was so damn embarrassed. I ended the call by saying, "Next time you have a problem, I would appreciate the courtesy of being told first; I would give you that same courtesy as well." And come to find out, Kyle (who was also a person of color) wasn't even doing anything to her; she just didn't like how direct he was when dealing with her. He was a little rough around the edges. That day, everyone learned a valuable lesson in office politics and managing behavior. If you let some white people take over story time, then you might never get to the bottom of the BS. I ended that call with a smile on my face, because I felt like the kid in one of those Pull-Ups commercials, saying, "I'm a big kid now."

Riding the Wave

Learning to manage office politics will make you a better leader and manager and help you preserve your sanity. Whether you should align with someone, like the characters on *Survivor*, or whom you should schmooze with at the holiday party—all can be scary, exciting, and downright exhausting. The sooner you understand the dynamics of the office, the better off you will be. And you have to understand that the workplace is not created equal! Women of color and underrepresented groups are sometimes at a disadvantage. Many of us don't have relatives who worked in corporate environments who could give us the handbook before we started, so a lot of it is on-the-job training—and it makes understanding the workplace that much more imperative for us. In 2017, a refreshing hashtag called #blackwomenatwork went viral (shout-out to Brittany Packnett), black women took to the social media streets and started discussing what it's like to be a black woman at work, and the stories weren't pretty. It was a beautiful display of community and shared experiences. If you were a black woman reading the tweets, you finally realized that you weren't the only one getting treated like crap at work.

Now That You Know

Office politics is one of those systems that have shut many women of color out of positions that we should have had a long time ago. Those same politics might also be what gave us a leg up, if we had the right workplace alliances. I am sure I have benefited along the way! Maybe you didn't know there was this alternate universe taking place inside organizations that you weren't aware of, and now that you are, you know how to position yourself going forward. In a perfect world, I would like to think we, as women of color, could use our influence for good. Meaning, when we hold influence within our companies because of our status, we can bring other women of color along with us. White men do it for their college buddies all day long. You know, the classic hostile takeover, and they become the CEO and they hire their frat brother Jim to be CFO and he doesn't even know that Quickbooks exists. There are no rules in office politics. But how can we use them to rewrite the narrative? The more we secure our seats, the better!

Remember to be strategic when aligning yourself with co-workers, and don't forget that you have to make choices for yourself that you won't need to spend tons of money on therapy to correct later down your career path. Keep your third eye open because not all workplaces are created equal. I know the game is exhausting and we are tired of playing it, but we have to play it long enough for a takeover (smile)!

Side note: I realize that some of you will choose not to get tangled up with office politics. You would be well within your rights to say, "Nah, homie, that isn't for me!"

With everything women of color already deal with at work just to gain a little respect, I can't help but fear the future of the workforce for women of color. Women of color have been dealing with so much shade that many are leaving the workforce altogether to start their own companies. If women of color leave the workforce before their time, I fear we won't influence the companies that need us most. On the flip side, when a woman's fed up, there ain't nothing you can do about it! I hope and pray to God, Jesus, and the Holy Spirit that the powers that be in the workforce get their stuff together and acknowledge what women of color bring to the table before we completely have our waiting to exhale moment and exit stage left while blaring good ole Mary singing, "I should've left yo' ass a thousand times." Just don't forget that you have options!

4

EVERYONE CAN'T BE A
GOLDEN GIRL

THE NIGHT HILLARY Clinton lost to Donald Trump, I was at the Javits Center with thousands of other supporters ready to break the glass ceiling. We were high-fiving and super geeked as if the Chicago Bulls had won another championship ring. I think I even spotted Katy Perry that night. Within hours it felt like the world was coming to an end. As the polls closed and the results rolled in, you could feel and see the tears starting to form in a room full of optimistic souls. Wait, what, we won't be having our first woman president? Needless to say, things didn't work out as planned. I woke up the next day feeling like I needed the hardest drink in the world. I remember walking to our neighborhood coffee shop, and the tension was so thick you could cut it with a knife. As I stood in line, there happened to be three black women behind me. They looked just as distraught as I did. I ended up buying whatever they wanted as my way of showing solidarity. If a few bagels and some lattes could ease the pain for ten minutes, I was down for the cause.

Over the next few days, it was like a sucker punch in the gut to find out that, among white women, a large majority voted for Trump rather than for Clinton. And 94 percent of black women slowly entered a sunken place, because we voted for HRC as if our lives depended on it. How the hell could white women have done the unthinkable to this country? Is this not my country 'tis of thee, sweet land of liberty? I am scared that freedom might not ring as loud as it used to. I was mad that night, and let's be honest, I am still not over it! And when white women had the opportunity to redeem themselves on the night of December 12, 2017, in Alabama, they blew it again. You remember that race, right? There was a special election to fill a Senate seat, and the front-runners were Roy Moore and Doug Jones. Thank Gawd, Doug Jones won, though 63 percent of white women voted for Moore (Trump's guy). And guess how many black women voted for Jones: 98 percent. I will never understand why white women continue to play themselves when it comes to supporting women's and human rights, by voting for candidates who want to strip rights away from women and underserved communities.

That same year, record numbers of white women wearing pink pussy hats attended the Women's March in 2017. As I marched in D.C., I kept wondering how many white women marching that day had voted for Trump. I was in full side-eye mode. The math just didn't add up. There was an iconic photo from the women's march of Angela Peoples, taken by her friend Kevin Banette, that read, "Don't forget: White Women Voted for Trump." And let me tell you—I have not forgotten, and I don't think other women of color have either! Even though I am not the keeper of all things for the culture, it's safe to say that women of color continue to be disappointed in white women today. Many claim to be allies and advocates, but when it's time to show some receipts, they are nowhere to be found. As the old saying goes, "Fool me once, shame on you, Fool me twice, shame on me!"

I will be the first to admit it: the Obama years spoiled me. I thought we could at least count on white women, if no one else. They are the same women adopting black babies and donating to communities of color. Where did things go wrong? After the election, I realized I had been living in a bubble for the last eight years and the strain between white women and women of color didn't just happen overnight. There has been a strained relationship since black women were forced to step foot on their plantations in 1619. Later, during Jim Crow, many white women made false accusations about people of color, which resulted in lynchings. Women of color raised their white children but weren't good enough to walk through their front door. Or when Shirley Chisholm ran for president in 1972 and her friend and feminist icon Gloria Steinem chose not to support her but instead endorsed Shirley's opponent George McGovern. And I would be remiss if I didn't mention something a little more current: when Nancy Pelosi had the audacity to speak against her black colleague Maxine Waters to the media. You don't have to be Sherlock Holmes to piece together these crimes. White women are consistently showing us who they are, and we just won't take them at their word. And these aren't isolated accounts from 200 years ago; this is happening each and every day.

The problem is, we are seeing this behavior played out not just in politics, but in the workplace as well. The empathy gap between white women and black and brown women is wider than ever. I think about my close white women friends—if I asked them to come march for black women, I don't think many of them would show up. If I asked them to come show up for me, that's a different story. They don't see how the two are connected. Shameful! It's one thing for them to tell me they have my back, and it's another thing for them to show me that they have my back. There are only a select few I have ever seen take a stand against police brutality or show solidarity for Black Lives Matter. White men and women I considered to be like family were posting about their support of Trump, without an ounce of empathy for what people of color in the United States might be feeling. They just echoed that "both sides" bull crap!

In order for white women to mend their broken relationship with women of color, they must first admit to their racist tendencies and lack of solidarity and lean into being better allies. White people have to acknowledge their hand in this country's systemic racism. And to be clear, I am not calling all white people racist, but I am calling many accomplices. An accomplice, by definition, is someone who helps another commit a crime. When folks don't stand up against racism, then I consider them accomplices. You can't support me and remain silent! And for the record, accomplices can no longer stand behind the lame excuse of "I don't see color." What do you do at a stoplight? I think it's time to explore the relationship of white women and women of color over time and dissect its current state as it pertains to the workplace, because I am having a hard time trusting white women to do the right thing. I am optimistic that we will find our way back into each other's arms, but in the meantime, let's pause any more marching together until we figure this thing out.

Small-Town White Folks

I began to think about my relationship with white women over the years, and I was reminded of the first time I remember encountering racism. I was in junior high school, and she was my teacher for science and arts classes. She would single me out in class, and I had no idea why. Until seventh grade, all of my teachers had been white, except for one, Mrs. McDaniels in third grade. And I was used to being the only black girl in most of my classes; I would have been shocked had it been any different. I was too young to comprehend why she didn't treat me like the other kids. It never once dawned on me it was because of the color of my skin. I was a good student, played on the basketball and track teams, and held a position on the student council board. In science class, I was the only black girl. In art class, I was one of two black girls, and she singled us out there too. It got so terrible that my dad had to come to the school. She wasn't ready for Larry! My dad is one of those black dads that *do not play* when it comes to his kids! I would go home and tell my parents about the mistreatment, and they had a long talk with me about racism. To this day, I am not even sure what my father said to her and the principal, but that teacher left me alone the rest of the year.

A year later, I had her brother as a teacher, and he didn't treat me much better. That same year, my best friend, who happened to be white, jokingly called me a tar baby. Also, I was invited to a birthday party that I couldn't attend; when I called my friend (a white girl), I overheard her mom say, "She talks so proper for a black girl," and then her mother laughed. It was the first time in my life that I was forced to see my color, not because I wanted to, but due to white women's ignorance. White men and women don't like to be called racist, even if they are racist. For years, my feelings would go ignored because their response was always, "I don't see color." And if you want to know the cheat code for unlearning racism 101, you'd take that entire sentence out of your lexicon. That phrase will trigger any sane person of color at the drop of a dime. And like good ole James Baldwin wrote, "I can't believe what you say because I see what you do." At a young age, I had to learn not to take everything white women did to me personally, or I would probably have started therapy as a child. I mean, I did go to school with kids that had Confederate flags in their car windows and no one said one thing about that, but if kids of color came to school in Starter jackets, then they must be gang members. I have been living my entire life with bias and racism, and I was told not to speak about it because "That's just the way it is!" And for so long, I accepted that narrative but, that no longer works for me—it's time to talk about our dirty laundry. I gotta testify!

Post-Racial, Huh?

There used to be this rumor that we were living in a post-racial America, which meant racism no longer existed. Now let's be clear, white people were the ones that started this rumor because a black man was elected president. This rumor made it difficult for people of color to claim that inequalities inside and outside the workplace were due to racism. Regardless of pre- or post-racial anything, racism existed before Obama and it's living its best life at the moment. Racism today becomes problematic only when you call it out. If I were to call a white woman at work a racist because she demonstrated behavior that warranted that response, I would be the one put on trial, not her. All she has to say is, "No, I'm not. You're just using the 'race card.'" For decades white men and women have been able to retaliate and demonize people of color for even insinuating they might be capable of displaying racism at work.

For women of color there is an imaginary line, and if we cross it and label someone racist or prejudiced at work, we might as well kiss our careers good-bye. It's the kiss of death to air our racial grievances. We don't have the luxury of using "race cards" unless they are absolutely necessary, and often, we just keep quiet about it and take the beating—because it's too arduous of a fight. How in the hell are we supposed to create a good working relationship with white men or women under these constraints? We aren't even given the space to vocalize our experiences, and white people discredit them when race is involved. In the words of Solange, "We got a lot to be mad about!" But again, white people would first have to acknowledge their role in this sh—show, and therein lies the problem! They do not want to be held accountable for their actions. Just because you didn't actively participate in slavery doesn't mean you haven't perpetuated the same generational stereotypes, ideas, and behaviors.

In my formative years when I experienced sporadic micro-aggressions from white women, I still held them in the highest regard. One would think I had Stockholm syndrome. It was white women who gave me my first two jobs out of college. A white woman was the first to invite me on a boat to jet ski. And a white woman helped me secure a book deal. I would be lying if I said, "All white women suck." On the other hand, I've experienced the worst moments of my career due to white women in the workplace. As a teenager, I learned the hard lesson that no person of color is exempt from racism, and as an adult, I relearned the same lesson. There is no magic number of white women friends that can bridge the racial divide.

Historically, the workplace has had a limited number of seats at the table for women and even fewer for women of color. Some women can't handle there being more than one woman at the table; they like being the only one. You see this regardless of race or age, and I'm sure it's timeless. I picture Harriet Tubman having to set some women straight on the path down the Underground Railroad. I am sure countless women were hating on Harriet, but she had to break it down for them: freedom or nah?

Most women have dealt with a "mean girl" or two, starting from their first day of school. I remember my first day at a new school, after my family moved from California to Illinois. I met a white family in the neighborhood who had a daughter my age, Amy, who later became one of my best childhood friends.

Amy welcomed me into her larger group of other white girl-friends. They just so happened to be the "popular girls." Those girls looked overjoyed to make a black friend. I was overjoyed to make some friends—everybody wins! This would be my introduction to how mean white girls could be. A few weeks later, one of the leaders of the group just up and decided to cut ties with some of the other girls in the group. These girls grew up together; some were even neighbors. I will never forget how those girls were no longer invited to sit at the "cool table" at lunch. I was new and had no allegiance to any of them, but it was the saddest thing I had ever seen: BFFs one day and out in the cold the next. And they never looked back! Cold as ice. That's when I knew, Beckys ain't to be effed with! I had never experienced anything like it. It was a fast lesson for me in white women and how shaky their loyalty can be. If they could be that calculated before they had a driver's license, then you better watch out when they make it to twenty-one!

Unfortunately, some of those mean girls grow up to become mean women, and some of those mean women become mean coworkers. In my career, I've worked with amazing women, some of the most caring and intelligent women on the planet—women of all shades. Up until a few years ago, I couldn't relate to the "mean girl" or "racist" stories I heard happening in the workplace, but then it happened to me. I affectionately refer to these women as the "Nordstrom ladies." The women who wear dated matching pantsuits and think because they know how to pronounce niçoise, that they own Nordstrom instead of just shopping there. Unfortunately, again, my three worst experiences in the workplace came at the hands of white women, but I only have time to write about two!

Traveled Down the Road and Back Again

When I was in my early thirties, I took a new job on the other side of the country in order to advance my career. It wasn't the first time I made a strategic move for a closer seat to the C-Suite. On paper everything seemed like the perfect fit. I had two days of interviews with what seemed like everyone in the department. I could see myself as a good "culture fit." One important person was missing from my grueling interview process, "Kerry," who was someone I would have to work closely with. Everyone spoke very highly of her and how many employees aspired to be as successful as her.

I didn't meet Kerry until about a month after I started to work there. We spoke on the phone a couple of times, but she was rarely in the office due to her travel schedule. I think it's fair to mention that I was the only black woman on our team. During our early conversations there were no clear red flags. I had just uprooted my life to move to a new state, with no friends or family, and I was eager to rebuild my life on the East Coast and equally excited about my new position. Kerry was a lot older than me and had been working in our industry for quite some time. For those of you who don't know me, I am a team player, polite and hardworking—I let emotional intelligence guide the way, and I believe most people who've ever worked with me would say the same. In the over fifteen years of working in my industry, I've had very few conflicts with my colleagues, but when they've happened, they have been with white colleagues. I have never been in a fight, never flipped any tables (hello, Teresa Giudice) and never pulled any wigs (countless reality TV shows). Kerry was supposed to show me the ropes since I was the newest member of the team and we would be dividing the Southwest region. My manager articulated this partnership to me when I was hired. At first, I thought to myself, "Great! I finally get a woman mentor." I'd never had a female mentor in the past who performed the same job function and with double my tenure. I guess you could say I created this harmonious partnership in my head with Kerry before she had a chance to accept. It was kind of like Cynthia and NeNe's friend contract in *The Real Housewives of Atlanta*; I wanted that with Kerry. It turned out to be the opposite of anything harmonious—more like disastrous. I would never have imagined she would try to make my life a living hell. In her defense, I don't believe she planned to treat me badly, but she did!

So back to the beginning: I figured that in order for me to be successful, collaboration would be the name of the game. I also wanted her to know that I wasn't coming to tread on her territory, so I played second string until I felt I was up to speed. I respected her tenure but she was not my manager; we were on the same team. Together, I hoped we'd conquer the world, like *Pinky and the Brain*. Not too long after I got up to speed, our new working relationship became a nightmare. The warning signs were subtle at first. You know the signs: being dismissive, cc'ing people on emails that have no business being cc'd, and going to my manager instead of coming to me. I wanted to give her the benefit of the doubt, yet this was not the same woman all my white colleagues raved about. Initially, I didn't want to attribute her actions to race, but there was nothing else, in my mind, that would make sense to attach these issues to. It began to get so bad that I would have panic attacks before going to bed because I knew I would have to go to work in the morning and she would probably start some stuff. You know someone is powerful when she is not even in the office every day, yet she still manages to be divisive. I allowed her to break my confidence (and it took me a while to get it back)! It was rare that I would go one week without some BS that seemed to include her! I was confused because I had never experienced this behavior before. Was Kerry really trying to push me out, or was I making this up? I felt like I was going crazy. Have you ever felt this way?

I believe this is a common line of internal questioning women of color go through in the workplace when we experience racism. We want so desperately for "it" not to be racism, so we start to make up excuses for white people, and it even leads us to question ourselves. The thing is . . . we all know when we are being mistreated, but we still try and cover up the bad behavior. We still try and push through the micro-aggressions; we do this because we are often working as "the only," and when you are in isolation, you don't have anyone to validate your feelings. We have been telling ourselves white people mean well since we were in grade school, when deep down we knew the truth. Eventually, that narrative starts to shape your identity. It's a hard-knock life for us! And this narrative was playing out for everyone to see, starring Kerry and co-starring me.

Things quickly spiraled past subtle, and we headed right into blatant racism. Many of my issues with her started to point to race. After my first few months on the job, Kerry asked me if I was hired to work with all the minority clients. I was taken aback. Oh, because I am black I must be here for all the blacks. Attention, "all the blacks": they have hired me to be your liaison; you are so lucky! What a small-minded woman. I told her I wanted to have the opportunity to work with all the clients just as she did. That was one of many microaggressions to come. How would you feel if you went to work each day and were constantly reminded that you are black and a black woman at that? And not in a black girl magic type of way! Maybe you know all too well. There wasn't enough black girl magic to prepare me for what was to come. I quickly had to grow a thick skin. Oh and prayer . . . lots and lots of prayers! In my new role, I was acutely aware of my race at every turn. I was referred to as "the black girl" on many occasions. Another layer of this bad Kerry sandwich was that many of her friends were also white women in our office who held executive positions. The disrespect eventually led to them mistreating me too. It is important to mention I was the only professional black female consultant at the firm. I was credentialed, good at my job—I belonged in my role just as much as anyone else on our team. There were other white women on our team who got along great with Kerry and me, separately. The issue was that they weren't dividing their territories, like Kerry and me, and they weren't black. Why would they bring me all the way to the opposite coast if no one was going to have my back? I didn't know how this ugly game would end, but I knew I had no chance at winning. I think I prayed the serenity prayer on the hour: "God grant me the serenity to accept the things I cannot change, courage to change the things I can, and wisdom to know the difference."

It Got Worse

There was one exchange with one of Kerry's BFFs that I remember as if it happened yesterday. I got a call asking if I had attended a certain event in Sarasota, Florida. I told her no, I wasn't in Sarasota that night; I was in New York City. She questioned me for over five minutes about where I said I was that night. I responded by saying, "I think I know where I was; why do you continue to question me as if I am lying to you?" She said that one of her clients had told me as if I am lying to you?" at the event, and she wanted to follow up with me because she works with them. I asked her if they called me by name. Her response was no, but they said they spoke to a black girl. The conversation then took an even more ridiculous turn. She said, verbatim, "You're the only black girl in the office, and I was trying to think of all the black girls they could have spoken with, and I figured it was you. If it wasn't you, what other black girls are over there?" I had never been so mad at work in my entire career. Every time she said "black girl," I wanted to show her what happens when you push a "black girl" to her limits. Come to find out, it was a black woman in another department who is an assistant. I asked my colleague how she would feel if I called her office and asked to speak to the "white girl" and to talk to her about all the "white girls" that worked in her department. Get the hell out of here with this. I managed, by the grace of God, not to cuss her out, but I did let her know it was inappropriate for her to approach me in this way and to call me a black girl—I am a black woman, you witch! Okay, I didn't say "witch," but I did say the rest. Jesus was indeed my fence that day! This is just one of the daily taxes on my emotional well-being I had to deal with in my office. She apologized, but she can save it for the next "black girl."

I was working with racist white women in a toxic work environment, and just when I thought it couldn't get any worse, it did! Each morning before I got out of my car, I would have to give myself a pep talk. Imagine showing up to work with internal armor to protect yourself from microaggressions and racism on any given day. I relocated for this position thousands of miles away, for a higher title and more pay, but I didn't read the racist fine print: *Hey Minda, in addition to your high salary, you will also be reminded of your place in this world; that you are a black girl in a predominantly white office.* I imagine this might be the same feeling former Republican National Committee chair Michael Steele felt when he heard his party only appointed him because he was black.

It was humiliating going through this because I felt like I didn't have anyone I could tell or anyone who could do anything about it. I was used to being "the only one" at work, and honestly, I began to think my entire career might be this way. I had always been able to navigate workplace politics with finesse. This experience subjected me to a different form of isolation, one that left me with no allies. As a form of protection, I began to stay out on the road as often as I could so I wouldn't have to be in the office. Even though my emails still dripped with racism from Kerry and her minions, at least I didn't have to see them. For an entire year, I had panic attacks. In meetings where she was physically present or was on the phone, I would experience an anxiety attack so bad that I could sometimes barely speak. It's hard for me to admit to you that my mental and physical health started to deteriorate, right before my eyes. I no longer felt like myself, and the scary part was I wasn't sure what to do about it; I couldn't just quit. Or at least, I felt like I couldn't. I felt like I had to tough it out, because that's what we do as women of color (meh). I have always been a high achiever and fondly thought of, but this environment wasn't set up for me to win. It was clear that Kerry wanted to be the only consultant in our territory. I found myself between a rock and a hard spot.

My One Wish

I couldn't even go to the human resources department because my rep was one of Kerry's BFFs. I felt like I was in an episode of *Black Mirror*. The one thing I wish I would have done sooner is address the situation with Kerry. When you find yourself in a similar situation, you have to advocate for yourself and not let people like her get away with murder. Maybe it would have worked, maybe not. That I will never know. But, to be honest with myself, I have to admit I gave Kerry way too much power early on. Because of her tenure, I kowtowed to her, and she used that to her advantage. I showed up as the grateful black woman, just happy to be in the building—that was my first mistake. I let her affect my career and my mental health. I should have demanded more from my supervisor to handle the situation and advocate for me; I should have taken my grievance to HR regardless of who was at the helm. I should have fought like hell for myself.

Even if I couldn't change the culture, I would have had my sanity, instead of picking up the pieces as I walked out their doors forever. Plus, I should have fought harder so the next woman of color wouldn't have to fight as hard. If I had done that, maybe there would be some documentation on the books, a paper trail. If there was a Yelp review for jobs, you already know which star they would get! And all jokes aside, I can't speak for the entire company being a horrible place to work; I can only speak to the department I worked in. No one woman or man should have that much power.

I shouldn't have waited a year to fight the system. It only hurt me in the long run. It is one of my biggest career regrets. Please don't make the same mistake that I did. Like the subway signs in New York City, when you see something, say something! Additionally, I could have left sooner. I didn't have to stay and be the strong black woman and hope for the best. I let my pride get in the way because I left my former employer for a pasture I thought was greener. I felt I had to make this work. This was mistake number two: you don't have to make everything work. You can leave if you are being mistreated because it doesn't get any better. I am reminded of a quote by Pauli Murray, "Black women, historically, have been doubly victimized by the twin immoralities of Jim Crow and Jane Crow. Black women, faced with these dual barriers, have often found that sex bias is more formidable than racial bias." The pride that I was so protective of? I was picking up the pieces of it scattered throughout the office day by day, inflicted by the Jane Crows who were my colleagues.

When Your Back's Against the Wall

I experienced the unthinkable for over a year before I privately asked Kerry if she had a problem working with me.

She immediately deflected and tried to make it seem like I was overreacting. It was a turning point in my career, and as a woman in an abusive work relationship, I had to ask myself if a seat at the table was worth the fight. Not every table is the right one—only you can make that call. At some point the proving and fighting to be seen and respected in an all-white environment becomes too much. When you're working in toxic environments, it's hard not to lean out. Deciding to stay or go is something that many of us battle each day. The final straw came after countless acts of blatant disrespect, from emails to phone calls to attempts to undermine my work. I tell this story not so you will feel sorry for me. I am showing you how systemic and institutional racism mixed with office politics work. Once you know how the game is set up, you will be better off. I dealt with this woman misbehaving for longer than I should have. I didn't want to accept that this job was not the right fit. I was fed up, and I was forced to stand up for myself. Women of color are always told not to rock the boat at work, especially when you are the only one. If rocking the boat means standing up for yourself, rock the hell out of the boat! "Don't rock the boat" is one of the worst pieces of advice, but it keeps getting passed down. If you don't prioritize your self-worth in the workplace, then you can't expect anyone else to.

I know what you're thinking: could things get worse? Of course they did! Eventually, things got so bad that my direct supervisor encouraged me to go to the department head. Side note: in a normal workplace, my direct supervisor would have also been Kerry's supervisor, but she didn't want him as her supervisor (he was an Indian man), and she reported directly to the department head. I had a meeting with the department head; let's call her "Tina." It was the most uncomfortable conversation I have ever had in my life. I think I'm still experiencing PTSD. The entire experience has left some scarring. I finally got the courage to discuss a year's worth of conflict, and Tina told me, "Kerry has been here a long time, the clients love her, and you need to suck it up. She isn't going anywhere." I proceeded to say, "I don't want her to go anywhere. I just want to be treated accordingly." She then told me, "This is unfortunate because you're doing a great job, and we hired you because we thought you had tough skin. You need to decide if this is the place for you." At that moment, I knew more than ever that it was not the place for me. In my perfect dream sequence, I would have said, "You can have all the damn seats, because you don't deserve me at your table," walked out, and slammed the door. Of course, I did not do that. The complete opposite! It took everything in me not to break down and cry in her office. I was so broke down emotionally that I was pretty fragile by the time I made it to her office. I mean, woman to woman, this is your response? Did I not endure enough and this is how you respond to me. I gave my two weeks' notice and walked out of her office with my head held high. About thirty minutes later, I had three voice messages from Kerry, demanding I call her back. If you hadn't guessed, Tina immediately called Kerry to tell her about our confidential meeting, and she wanted to discuss it with me. How inappropriate and unprofessional could Tina have been? I chose not to engage Kerry, and I didn't return her calls.

In a sheer panic, she finally emailed me and cc'd a bunch of people who had nothing to do with the situation—to save face. One of the items that I discussed in the meeting with Tina was database management. Before I was hired, I kept hearing Kerry liked working with newbies on ways to slice the data and identify new clients. She included that I was too senior for her to spend time with me on reporting. Since I didn't return her calls—as if she thought I was going to subject myself to any more of her BS—she wrote me this email. I still have it, as proof that I wasn't making up these stories and to remind myself of how I made it through the fire. She wrote me this long, drawn-out email, popping off about the stress she had been under due to some family situation, and even with that family situation, she still was able to perform at a high level. Then she wrote something about how it was not her responsibility to hold my hand. Let's pause here. How does showing a new person the ropes in a territory you're familiar with manifest into me wanting her to hold my hand? I wanted her to transfer the institutional knowledge she had about our shared territory. That was something I asked for on day one, and I think it was a reasonable request. She went on to demean me as a senior professional for inquiring about ways to work collaboratively. Remember those passive-aggressive ways I spoke about? This is a perfect example. Whew . . . if I could share those emails with you, you would be livid. And I think I might be paraphrasing a lot kinder than she was to me! Again, everything that I said to Tina, Kerry wrote me in email form. She went on to write me a novel about how supportive she thought she was and even took credit for a project I executed. She even took it a step further and offered to refer me to an all-black consulting firm if I wanted another position. Some white women are so effing tone deaf. She couldn't even own her part in driving me out of my position and then played the hero and offered a connection to an all-black consulting firm. Girl, bye! I had a going-away party in the office, and neither of them showed up. And these women were "leaders" of the lean-in group at work. Just let that all of that sink in! I don't think that was the leaning in Sheryl had hoped for.

Suffering in Silence

In this particular work environment, I dealt with racism on various levels, and because several white women participated in this toxic behavior it created a toxic work environment. My supervisor was a Indian man, and he was experiencing his own trauma. He too had moved to take a new position that would advance his career. About a year after we both left, we were able to laugh over a drink and compare war wounds.

I mention some of the actions I wish I had taken sooner because my hope for you is that you will diplomatically and respectfully stand up for yourself. I thought my work alone would make Kerry treat me like an equal. I didn't want to accept that she had racist tendencies. I thought the situation would fix itself, but it only got worse. I was going to fail because I had women like her at the helm. When I was going through this, I had a lot of men and women in my office secretly confirming I was being mistreated and commending me for my strength. None of them ever stood up for me in public (workplace politics). Remember when I mentioned white people being accomplices? I am not sure what hurt more, being mistreated or being mistreated while everyone stood by and watched it unfold. Sadly, I felt validated when they would come to me to privately commend me because it meant I wasn't making this sh— up in my head, yet it didn't fix the damage that was done. I had other white women on my team that could have stood up for me, and they too failed me, just as Kerry did. The late activist Ella Baker gave a speech in 1968; on racism, she said, "The future of our culture—our country, depends not so much on what black people do, as it does depend on what white people do. Now, this is a hard lesson for some of us. That the choice as to whether or not we will rid the country of racism, is a choice that White America has to make."

The Aftermath

It's been many years since, and I regularly read about this company in the news for some racist shenanigans. Clearly it wasn't just my department, but a workplace culture. In hindsight, I see what I could have done differently before it got to the point of no return. There was a deadly cocktail of racism and a toxic work environment. I am by no means saying that all white women create a toxic working environment, but in this case many of them exacerbated the situation. The lack of diversity was frightening. Knowing what I know now, I wouldn't take another job that doesn't value people of color. For a long time I didn't know my supervisor was experiencing a similar situation with Tina. So he was in no shape to advocate for anyone. There was early gossip chatter about these ten white women in the office running everything. I don't know how I would have known that during the interview process, but I could have asked about my predecessor.

When I interviewed, I didn't ask many questions about the team, or perhaps I didn't ask the right questions. I want to impress upon women of color: please make sure you interview your future employer. Interviewing happens on both sides. And if you are one of the only people of color in the office, you have to ask those tough questions as well. Here are a couple of starter questions to read the room: What is the work culture like? What steps are in place to increase diversity? Additionally, ask questions about leadership style and hierarchy. As you start to uncover some of the foundational questions, drill down into the team dynamics. A few to consider during your next interview: Can you tell me who I will be working closely with? What are the team's strengths and challenges? Has the company changed since you've joined? These are some of the questions I wished I had asked, but I am glad I am able to pass them along to you! It's up to you to cover all your bases; they will not show you the skeletons in the closet. And if you find that the answers don't sit well with you, run for the hills. After leaving my position, I found out that there was another woman of color in the position before me. And since I left, a few more women of color have left my old position. It's like a bad scene in *Get Out*. There is no amount of money and no title that will replace your peace and overall career health, so do your due diligence. With regard to Kerry, not only did I deal with racism, but she was a bully too. And I don't give a damn how many black friends she said she has. My experience with her was flat-out racism. A racist bully is good for no one, and shame on that company for allowing her and others like her to drive out good talent. Attention all women: Workplace bullying goes on because no one steps in to stop it or offers support to the victim. When you see woman-on-woman crime at work, give that woman some comfort and give her this book. As women, we can only advance in a male-dominated workplace if we stick together. But, if you observe this type of behavior, be the hero you'd wish someone would be for you. And if it happens to you—well, time to be your own hero!

Thank You for Being a Friend

One of my favorite authors, Audre Lorde, wrote a letter in 1979 to a white woman named Mary Daly. It can be found in her book *Sister Outsider*. This exchange between the two is one that I believe summarizes the strain that still stands between white women and women of color. In one line Audre wrote: "This letter has been delayed because of my grave reluctance to reach out to you, for what I want us to chew upon here, is neither easy or simple. The history of white women who have been unable to hear black women's words, or to maintain dialogue is long and discouraging." She went on to write, "But in order to come together, we must recognize each other." This is the true story of women of color and white women, picked to work together, to find out what happens, when people stop being polite and start getting real! I know women of color and white women aren't the golden girls. I don't expect we'll sit out on the lanai and drink tea, but dammit, can't we all just get along! I have never looked at a white woman as a threat. I love to see us collaborate and support one another, so when it doesn't happen, I take it personally. It's time for all sides to finally address and acknowledge that this beef is way past its expiration date. Women of color have been waiting for white women to take responsibility for their passive-aggressive nature, specifically when interacting with us in the workplace. Let's keep it 100 (real)!

I hope that white women will take the time to read this chapter. I know all of you don't act this way, but you might know some colleagues that do, and when you see inequalities taking place, you might help another woman out. I don't view all white women as enemies or as if they can't be trusted. But there are a lot I don't trust. I know firsthand how our relationship with white women can be strained. I naively thought white women could do no wrong at work, and I bought into that lie because some of the stories I had heard had not happened to me. White women have done a good job of not being seen as the villain. They helped create this narrative that white men are the ones we should fear at work. (We have our own history to reconcile with white men.) Just as they did on the plantation and during the Jim Crow era, they pass the buck on responsibility. Meaning they don't like to confront situations that arise head on; they like to make excuses, play the victim, and run away—oh, and often cry. When I conduct workshops across the country, I ask women of color who are the sponsors, mentors, or champions of their successes. The answer is white men almost 99 percent of the time. Many white women desperately claim to be allies, but frankly, most of them have not done much to help advance women of color in the workplace. How Sway?

Let me present the facts in a different way because that pill might be too hard to swallow. It's 2018, and we have no African American women as CEOs of any Fortune 500 companies. And we've only had one so far. In 2017 *Fortune* magazine wrote about twenty-three women CEOs, two of whom were women of color. I went to each of their executive leadership pages and out of all twenty-three women, only three of them have a black woman on their executive leadership team, one on each. Out of the twenty-three female CEOs, five of them have one black woman each on their boards. As of October 2018, there were twenty-five women CEOs, and none of them were black. So, I pose the question again, where are all these white women in pussy hats advocating for my success? The facts show that white women are not checking for us in the workplace.

My early work experiences with Kerry were the impetus for creating The Memo, and for that alone I am grateful. I realized that women of color need space to be able to talk about our relationship with white women, even if white women pretend nothing is wrong. Recently, I moderated a panel on "The Empathy Gap." This event was for white women and women of color. It was such a great event, but there weren't many white women in the room. The brave souls that did show up, I applaud for wanting to do the work. We must come together and talk about the hard stuff! White women, when you're ready to phone a friend—we will be ready to have this discussion. We don't want white women advocating for us until they own the history that led us to that large percentage who voted for Trump. You can't vote for a racist and then in the same breath tell me that you're not a racist and that women's rights are human rights.

I left the situation with the Nordstrom ladies (maybe that should have been a red flag all by itself) with some battle wounds and was able to bounce back with a position with even better pay and title—and a slightly better work environment. I sometimes wonder what the outcome would have been if I had had one or two white women as allies in that office. I did go to lunch and happy hour with white women in that office, but none of them had my back in a real way. Together we might have been able to take down the regime. I am sure many of you have stories like this, and it saddens me to think how many of us endure racism by white women who are supposed to be rooting for equality and equity. I hate that many of you went through your situation alone, without allies or support. This is why we have to speak up and demand respect, be it with white women or any other woman. After all the sleepless nights and bouts of depression, the experience made me stronger and pushed me to become an advocate for other women of color so you no longer have to question your sanity and feel like your voice is unheard. The bottom line is, women of color will be the majority of the workforce by the year 2060; if I were a white woman, I would *do better.*

5

NO MONEY, MO' PROBLEMS

THE PROPHETS PUFFY, Mase, and Biggie told us "the more money we come across, the more problems we see." I almost think it's the opposite—the less money we come across, the more problems we see. Especially if you live in a high-priced city like New York City, women need every single coin and nothing less. And when I reflect on the wage gap as it pertains to women of color, this statement rings true. As Queen Bey would say, "Gimme my check, put some respect on my check." Black and brown women fall on the lower end of the pay scale; anywhere from 43 cents to 69 cents to a white man's dollar. Asian women make around 83 cents and Caucasian women around 79 cents. What happened to equal pay for equal work? Please explain how I can sit in the cube next to Becky and do the same work and get paid less? Someone sound the alarm; this would not go over well in Wakanda! And even if black and brown women never negotiate their salaries or ask for more, which is one reason often given for why we make less—even if that is true, companies are still getting away with underpaying women of color. And as far as I am concerned, this logic doesn't make any damn sense. What I will say is, once I found out I could negotiate my salary, you best believe I upped the ante. We have to start asking; no more doing work for anything less than market value. It can be uncomfortable to talk about money, but it's even more uncomfortable when you have to dodge the bill collectors because you don't have enough income to pay your bills. And, it's unfair to you to work over forty hours a week and not bring home enough money to cover your expenses. Not earning enough should make you mad as hell! In this chapter I hope you find the strength and your voice to ask for more. Or at the very least, do some investigative work to make sure you're not being underpaid. For hundreds of years our ancestors worked for little to no money, and when they left the plantation, there was no gold watch waiting for them, no 401k, and there sure weren't any cost-of-living adjustments. They worked twenty times harder than we have, too; so for their sacrifice alone, b— better have our money!

The Wage Gap. Equal Pay Day. Black Women's Equal Pay Day. Whoever else's Equal Pay Day. It's all BS. If white women cared about my salary, they would stop saying women make what "they" make. Don't act like you're advocating for me when you know you're not. If you want to play the role, then take a pay cut until all women make the same. Until then, don't talk to me about a wage gap or give me your tips to achieve parity. While you're living your best life, I am trying to figure out how to make ends meet. And don't get me started on the men. Women of color shouldn't have to do a full-on PowerPoint presentation to reach parity. Me and my sistas should not have to conduct another case study with pretty charts or write an essay on the inequalities of the wage gap. It pisses me off when we call businesses out on the carpet about the wage gap, and their favorite line is "we are working on it." By doing what, exactly? I might need a master class on why you can't pay everyone starting out at the same base salary and work from there. And if all the white men in the world were doing phenomenal work compared to women of color, then I would be the first one to wave the surrender flag, but I am sure that isn't the case at each company. And let's be fair—women calling out white men for their mediocrity is lame. It's not their fault employers are being shady AF. Now if white men and women are leading these companies and have the power to close the wage gap, then we have the right to point the finger, not just because they are white but because they are the majority and they hold positions of power. If black women held all the keys to cracking the equal pay code and chose not to, I'd point my finger at us too! For example, the current CEO of Salesforce, Marc Benioff, is using his platform and privilege to talk equal pay for equal work for men and women. He is using his privilege to make the change. A CEO taking on the wage gap is the type of movement we need from anyone in a position of privilege. If Salesforce can do it, so can others. With that said, open your Bibles, turn to the book of Rihanna, stand up for the reading of the scripture "Pay me what you owe me," and let the church say, "Amen!"

In 2018, Nielsen came out with a study that says African American women will reach $1.5 trillion in buying power by

2021, which is higher than any other demographic. This report signals to me that my dollar matters—when it comes to being a consumer of goods. Some of these same companies that take our money for goods and services think it's okay to value us as consumers but undervalue us as producers. When I was in college, there was a white girl who lived in the same dorm, and she would run down the hallway and end her sentences with the phrase "That's horsesh—." At the time, I wasn't sure where that mantra fit into my life, but it seems very applicable now. Companies are fine with women of color going into debt over purchases we can't afford but don't want to pay us what we are worth to pay down that debt. There is no reasonable or ethical explanation for the unbalanced pay scale, and we must fight to see the change we want by starting with an ask. And that means asking for more, whether it's your first job out of college or the last job you take before retirement. Own it! The statistics show that we have the power to affect various industries, which means that we also have to learn the power of making a strong ask that serves our personal bottom line. Throughout this chapter, you will learn strategies to negotiate money and fringe benefits. We will also discuss how to tap into knowing and owning your worth. Knowing your worth isn't just some cute mantra I want you to chant; I want you to get to a point where you know your worth internally. Knowing your worth will keep you from selling yourself short!

My Wonder Years

One of the first applications I filled out was for a position at Dairy Queen when I was fourteen or fifteen years old. I knew they paid minimum wage, which, at the time was less than five dollars an hour, yet they asked me to fill in my expected hourly wage. As if I had a choice! Why all these damn games, really, Dairy Queen? As a young girl with dreams of saving up for a car, I knew I was worth more than five dollars. I wrote in eight dollars and prayed for the best. Of course, the manager laughed at me and told me I could have the job for minimum wage. I didn't know negotiating was even a thing at that age, so I happily accepted my new position to make cookie dough blizzards and write congratulatory messages on frozen ice cream cakes. I wish I would have known about negotiation strategies at fifteen. I would have been killing the fast food industry! As the years went on, I would continue to write in more money on my applications, knowing I would get whatever they were offering up.

It wasn't until my first job out of college that I knew I had to ask for more, and receiving a "no" wasn't going to cut it. I was in my twenties, and no one had sat me down to discuss the wage gap; hell, I didn't even know there was one. I just knew I had to advocate for more money or I wouldn't be able to afford the studio apartment I had just signed the lease for in the Lincoln Park neighborhood of Chicago. I signed my lease at a property that gave me my first month free, and I knew my first paycheck had to cover the rent and utilities, and a few extra dollars for summertime Chi nights out with friends. I remember the company offered me $28,000, and I asked for $30,000. A small win, in my opinion, and more money than I had anticipated. As I began to make work friends, I started to hear what others were making. Some of us were doing the *exact* same job and receiving different amounts. Now, some of us were fresh out of college, and others had been working longer, but I was making more than some of the older women. I didn't understand why our salaries were all over the place, yet I was always left curious. I was making on the higher end, so I just left it alone. That is, until I was "promoted" to oversee a small group of administrative assistants while my manager was on maternity leave. I affectionately called her "bucket lady," because she kept a bucket at her desk that she would vomit into during her pregnancy. No judging! I was excited to have this newfound leadership position and asked my manager if I could have a stipend since I would be doing her duties and mine while she was gone. She took it up the flagpole and they said no and then came back and said I should split those duties with another colleague so they wouldn't have to pay me extra. This too is horsesh—! My so-called negotiation strategies were solely based on trial and error, but that's how I figured out all this salary stuff. Again, I wasn't asking for more because I wanted to change the wage gap; I still didn't know I was even negotiating. I was just looking at the situation from what I thought was a fair viewpoint. And I quickly realized that most things at work are never fair or ever balanced.

Fast forward about five years, and I was applying for a new job and transitioning from one career to another. This was the first time someone had discussed with me how you negotiate and ask for what you want—the proper way. I met this white man named Chuck, who turned out to be the mentor I never knew I needed. He was the first person who sat down with me and schooled me on how salaries work. The position I was applying for had a range of $63,000 to $80,000 a year. I didn't have the exact job experience, but Chuck taught me how to articulate what I had been doing and how to tell the story of how my skills were transferable. I figured I would ask for $63,000 because I was not qualified per their job description, and it was significantly more than I was making. Chuck stopped me dead in my tracks and said:

1. You can do this job.

2. There is a range for a reason.

3. Do you want to make 80,000?

4. Ask for more.

Chuck didn't tell me what I should ask for—he left that up to me—but he did give me some talking points for when the money talk came up. God, I am forever grateful to Chuck for that advice. Because if I had gone with the $63,000, it would have been hard to reach six figures as the years went on, due to incremental raises of up to 3 percent or not receiving one at all. I asked for $75,000, and I was scared sh—less. I didn't think I was worth it. They came back and offered $70,000, and I took it. And Chuck was right: even though I had never done that exact job, I soared. And I should have pushed for closer to $80,000. It was through that experience that I realized a couple of things: (1) I am my best advocate, and (2) negotiation happens on both sides. If you get nothing else from this story, I hope you know your worth before you start negotiating, because knowing your worth is powerful. And some of you might be wondering how to find your worth when you feel like you might not have much left. I told you in Chapter 1 to view me as your coach rooting for you at every step of the way, and now is no different. Do you know the difference between Vincent van Gogh and Michelangelo? Two words: belief and worth. Vincent van Gogh questioned being an artist because his father was not supportive of his career. That doubt hindered him from truly knowing his worth. Michelangelo had a similar type of father who tried to stop him from being an artist, but the thing is, he didn't let his father get in his way—he knew he was an artist and believed he was an artist. Side note: Michelangelo's father would punish him for painting, and that still didn't stop him because he knew what was inside him. Both men went on to produce legendary art, but only one always knew his worth. Think about the power we give away for our craft, and think about how much freedom you will feel when your talent is matched with your worth. And you have the power to advocate for what you make! Even if you think your skills don't match and it's a new position, figure out a way to articulate your current skills so that they coincide with the job requirements.

Lastly, I want to briefly touch on how to articulate your skill set if it is slightly different than the job description. For example, you might have spent most of your career working in a nonprofit organization, where you held the title of Development Associate. In your role you identified new donors, cultivated those relationships, solicited donors, and stewarded new and existing donors. After ten years of working in that role, you want to make a career transition into pharmaceutical sales. You start looking at various job descriptions, and initially you count yourself out because you don't have five to seven years of hard sales experience, although you could run circles around many of the soft skills in the job description. Breaking news: your current Development Associate position is essentially a sales position; you just call it fundraising in your industry. Often, the functions in the two jobs are the same, but they have different names because the industries are different. Now you can revise your résumé to reflect the decade of sales experience. Does that make sense? Doesn't that open up a lot of new possibilities in your career? Again, you get to take the power into your own hands! And, if you are negotiating for an internal position, keep reading to see how I address an experience with a former employer.

From Low-Income to Middle Class

Coming from a low-income family, I had never imagined earning $70,000. I remember thinking after college, if I could make $40,000 to $50,000, I would be rich. It was more money than my parents had ever earned (at the time). And women of color who "make it" feel this pressure (sometimes self-imposed and other times imposed by our families) to help take care of everyone else. Every time I ever asked for more, it was for my family and me. Can you imagine the stress of making $70,000 while your family back home is struggling to pay their rent? Black and brown women don't have the luxury of running off to Bloomingdale's; we work to try and carve out a piece of living our best life while making sure our families have what they need too. In 2017, the Institute for Women's Policy Research and National Domestic Workers Alliances reported that 80 percent of black mothers are their household's breadwinner, while only 50 percent of white women are their household's breadwinner. This is just one of the many reasons the wage gap upsets me. Many of us are the first people in our families to graduate from college, the first in our family to go from lower income to middle or upper-middle class. It's a wonderful feeling but comes with a lot of responsibility. Many of our families struggled for decades to overcome economic and social inequalities caused by inadequate access to education and housing and generations of incarceration. Black and brown women tend to hold their families up on their shoulders—so the entire family can advance. Our financial expectations aren't always discussed in the black community—it's another one of those unwritten rules that seem to guide the way women of color live their lives.

So when Becky makes $70,000, she gets to keep that (most of the time); she isn't worried about her family and sending money back home—she can plan a summer vacation with Kim and Suzy. And come to think of it, Becky might be receiving money from her family. Many of my white, wealthy adult friends still receive money from their parents.

So when our companies stick us for our paper, that hurts generations of women of color. Historically, women of color are taught family and church first. Those are our giving priorities. And after we take care of those things, there is little left. We need every last cent! Even though our families are working, many of them are barely making ends meet. So we can't turn our back on our families nor would we want too. But, if we made at least what our counterparts made, that would lessen our burden!

Not Just the Money

Over the years I learned that salaries aren't the only thing up for negotiation. We can negotiate extra vacation days, professional development stipends, remote working days, and stock options. I even had one woman tell me she negotiated flights back and forth to her preferred home on the weekends. Sometimes we are so darn focused on money that we don't get creative enough. About five years ago I went through the first negotiation that felt like work. And by then I knew my worth, and no one could tell me nothing, and I say this very humbly. Let me explain. I knew my work was stellar, and I brought a lot to the table. I had been through a couple of negotiations, so I understood how the game worked, but I have to be honest and admit it's been scary each time. Those nerves have never gone away for me! No two negotiations are the same, and you can't predict the outcome, but it does require preparation. You can't just walk in and say, "I want more money." For this negotiation, I had to be willing to put it all on the line. Meaning that regardless of their response, I had to be confident, prepared, and ready to make my request known.

I had been working for my employer for several years, and I was moving up the ladder, and I guess you could say I had achieved my seat at the table. I began to get comfortable with the access I had and the money I was making. Then a headhunter called me on the telephone. Because my field is niche, these calls would happen frequently, but I never planned on leaving to go somewhere else. That recruiter caught me at the right time and the right place. She wanted to discuss an opportunity with me. She said the organization's name, and it was the crème de la crème. Based on the name alone, I wanted to hear what she had to say. She went on to tell me that it would be a promotion and I would make significantly more than I was making now. And when I say significantly, babbbby, I mean *significantly*. The catch—I would have to relocate from one coast to another. Before that phone call, I probably wouldn't have considered another offer. I felt like I was in a good place in my career, and I thought my company was "taking care of me," and in many ways they were, but realizing what I could have and how this opportunity would get me closer to my long-term career goals gave me a new outlook. I was a little disappointed that I didn't have this same opportunity where I currently sat.

It was such a pivotal point in my life, because had that call not happened I might still be in that situation. It wasn't a bad one, but it wasn't going to position me in the long run to be where I wanted to be. This call gave me a healthy dose of reality, and I needed that. Sometimes we get too comfortable and need someone to hold up a mirror and remind us there's more. You might be in a good position, but what if I told you there might be a better one? Long story short, we had several conversations, and I flew out there for interviews. They were, as Drake said, "Talking my language," and at that point, I didn't need the Rosetta Stone to understand it meant more money and a title change. Those two things were important factors to me. It was one of the hardest decisions I've had to make career-wise. I liked the job I had, and my social circle was intact. I have always been someone gunning for the top, and I was starting to bump my head on the ceiling where I was. Taking this new job would give me everything I thought I wanted. And sometimes you have to relocate to open up new opportunities for yourself. This would be the second time I would take a position that required me to uproot my life and start over for a better career opportunity. And since I wasn't married and didn't have kids, I had the flexibility to see what's on the other side of this opportunity. And even if it didn't work out, I knew I owed myself this much to see what's possible for me. The hard truth was I knew I wouldn't get this new salary staying where I was, not anytime soon. It was the moment I stopped playing checkers with my career and leveled up past chess and went straight to the Chinese game Go.

Side note: Career choices aren't always easy and clear. Sometimes they work out as you planned, sometimes there are roadblocks, but as hard as we have worked to get to this point, you might as well play your best hand. And to be honest, we should put ourselves in positions to negotiate every now and then so we get more and more comfortable asking for what we want.

Chuck was there once again to help me strategize about my next steps. If my current company could give me what I wanted, then I wanted to stay. If they couldn't, then I had to pack up and leave. Before I started, I had to be clear on what I was willing to accept and be comfortable walking away. I could not afford to make empty promises or threats. Just because you have another offer won't always mean that your company will take the necessary steps to make a better offer. You might present another offer and they show you the door. It was apparent that I had to be willing to walk away once I entered into such a high-stakes negotiation—if things didn't go as planned. I want you to understand what is at stake for you, so be cautious if you decide to take the route I did. I entered into a serious negotiation, and I had no clue whether I would be happy at the end or unsatisfied. I had no control over what my current employer would agree to.

The potential new employer made me an offer, and I had a couple of days to come back and give them my answer. I went to my direct supervisor and told him I had an offer. I explained that I hadn't been out searching for a new job, yet this opportunity that had come up positioned me closer to my career and financial goals.

Let's take a beat, and discuss how my short-term and long-term goals played into my negotiation decision and strategy. Hopefully, it will add some context for my decision-making process. Money wasn't the only thing that mattered to me. As I mentioned earlier, this new company was offering money and a title change. The type-A part in me always has a running list of my short- and long-term career and personal goals. I had hit most of my short-term goals, such as serving on committees, staffing senior leadership, and traveling for work. But I still had a long way to go with my long-term goals: six-figure salary (I was close), senior title, and a certain amount of dollars raised (bragging rights in my fundraising role). I knew if I stayed at my current organization, it would probably take another one to three years to reach those long-term goals. And my current workload was that of someone in a senior position, minus the pay and the title. This potential opportunity would allow me to have all three in the next thirty days. The upward mobility was important to me, even if that meant I had to relocate.

My advice to you is this: when you face a similar career-changing event, make sure your moves are strategic and in alignment with your career blueprint (I will touch on career blueprints in the next chapter). If you haven't mapped out your short- and long-term goals, I would start creating your list now. It doesn't have to be anything fancy, but at least you know you aren't just waking up every morning for the heck of it; you are strategically securing your seat!

Back to our regularly scheduled story, I asked if they would be able to at least match the offer. Let me pause here. I was so scared to have this conversation. I knew all the powers that be would be surprised by my news. I had never rocked the boat and always played by the rules. I had personal working relationships with many of the executive staff members, and I could have gone to them first, but I wanted to go up the appropriate channels. Of course, my supervisor was surprised. He immediately contacted his boss, and within a couple of hours I was in his office. I explained the situation and everyone acted so GD surprised. Why would they be surprised that I wanted more from my career? When I met with my direct manager's boss, he asked me point-blank what the offer was, and I told him. He laughed and said that he doubted the company would be able to do that, but he would ask. After several conversations with different executive staff members, they offered me a new title and a little more money, but the amount wasn't close enough to my new offer. I pushed for more money. They countered and said that they could give me half now and the other half in six months. So peep this: It went from "We can't do the money" to "We can do half now and half later." I said I needed to think about it and would let them know the next day, I chatted with my parents and Chuck, all of whom had different ideas about what my following steps should be, but all of them supported whatever decision I made. This was a hard decision to make. Three weeks before, I was going along with the status quo, thinking that it got no better than what I was doing. Even though I wasn't completely satisfied where I was, I accepted it. I was worried because in some twisted way, I felt that my current company had been loyal to me, providing me all of these leadership opportunities and resources. But, actually, I was the loyal one. I worked double time and should have had the title and the salary to match if they truly valued me. At this point, I couldn't put their needs before mine. This was my career, and when I stand before the career gods, I want them to say, "Well done, my child." Not "Girl, really, you know we had a better future for you, but you settled." Since my current company could not come correct, I decided to walk away and start my new job. I felt like the company that claimed I was a great asset wasn't willing to go the extra mile for me, so I decided to go the extra mile for myself.

In negotiations like this, you find out how loyal a company really is to you. I thought about all the traveling I did through-out the month for years, being accommodating at the drop of a dime, putting my career first at the expense of personal relationships. I felt I had given all I had to this company, and it stung that they couldn't do the same for me. They could have given me exactly what I asked for, but I think they thought I would fold because they knew how loyal I was. They knew how much I enjoyed my career. I once had a manager call me a "utility player" because I would play whatever role needed to be played. I learned so much about myself during this negotiation: that the twenty-three-year-old Minda would have never thought to push the envelope and make such a big ask. The Minda who thought she needed to put her head down and just do the work would never have taken the risk! And if I am being candid, the old me probably would have taken their half-assed bump and called it a day. But the thirty-two-year-old me had nothing to lose and everything to gain. I had given my employer so much power over my career decisions, but I finally took the power back! Never be afraid to take your power back! And like my girl Gwen Stefani said, "I ain't no hollaback girl," and neither are you.

I went on to accept my new position, new salary, and new state. During my first year, I would hear back from my old company on how they missed me and wished I would come back. They always left the door cracked in case I wanted to come back. It felt good: sometimes you have to leave for both parties to know what they had. The workplace is no different than a romantic relationship. All relationships have moments of functionality and dysfunction. A year later my old employer officially offered me my job back. Earlier in the book you learned that my new employer wasn't the best situation. It turned out to be hell on earth, just with more money and a new title. I never told my old employer about my current situation because in negotiations you can't always show your hand. We reentered negotiations, and this time my ask was much higher. I knew that if they were asking me to come back, I had leverage. I wanted a more senior title than I already had, and I asked for more money and negotiated being able to work remotely. Some of you might be thinking, *Hold up, Minda, you are getting greedy.* No, sis, I am getting everything that already belonged to me—had they done right by me the first time. And even though I hated my new job, I still knew my worth. All companies are looking out for their bottom line, so you have to always make sure you're looking out for your bottom line too. I didn't know what they would accept this time around, but once again, I had to throw it all on the table. The good news is that they accepted, and that, folks, is what I call a miracle. Side note: I would go on to receive three salary increases during my tenure. Never shy away from asking for what you want. You may not always get it, but at least you did your part. If I can do it, trust me, you can too.

What Does It Take?

Negotiating your needs and wants will require you to put on your big girl pants and own the ask. A nice transitional phrase might be, "I would like to discuss my compensation to bring it in alignment with the market value in [your company's city]." This is also a good time to mention that you've been researching the current market value of similar positions in your field. Research, research, research! You don't want to go into this conversation without doing the research. This will help your case for support and open the dialogue. Not to mention, it will signal to your boss that you did not come to play. The main ingredients in any negotiation are research, strategy, and confidence. You can't have one without the other two. I knew without a shadow of a doubt that I had the power during our last negotiation to ask for what I wanted. They could say no, but at least I made the ask. I already had a job, so if my old employer didn't want to come correct, it was no sweat off my brow. But the truth was just as much as they missed me, I missed them. We both had to leave the relationship to value the other person. Negotiations don't always work out like mine, but each of us has the opportunity to advocate for ourselves. And if we don't, honey, no one else will. And, let me be clear, I wasn't showing up to these negotiations like Sasha Fierce; I was showing up more like Michelle Williams in her first year in Destiny's Child. Eventually, through practice and preparation, I found my voice and was comfortable being Kelly Rowland. Never sleep on Kelly!

Recently, I had a conversation with another woman of color, and she told me her client had been paying her fee for over five years, and within the last couple of weeks the client notified her they would no longer be paying this fee and offered to pay half. The expectation was that she would still perform the same function. Let me get this straight, you used to pay me for a service, and now you want to cut the fee in half and still receive the same level of service? Where the hell do they do that at? This company is one of the most profitable healthcare systems in the country, and they want to underpay her for the same work. She tried to negotiate, and they wouldn't budge. She was not in a position to walk away. She needed that contract, so she planned to keep them as a client because the entire loss would be too much to recoup. I reminded her that if this company was once paying her a large amount, another company would compensate her at that amount and possibly more. Sometimes we talk ourselves out of the possibilities due to fear of the unknown.

I believe that when companies undervalue us in this way, it's a sharp reminder this company won't be loyal to us, and they will pull another stunt like this later. Why would you want to work for someone who doesn't see your worth? The way your company or potential company treats you during a negotiation is a telltale sign of how the relationship will play out. If they are being shady now, what makes you think they won't be shady later? And as women of color, we already deal with so much BS in the workplace that we don't have time to play around with our money. Always remember we have options too. I checked in with her a few months ago, and she had found another company that was willing to pay her almost twice as much as the shady one. Look at God!

Say Yes, to You

I have entered into a few negotiations a couple of times as an employee and as an entrepreneur. I am not an expert, but I have learned over the years never to sell myself short. I interviewed expert negotiation and leadership coach Jamie Lee for my podcast *Secure the Seat* about women of color and negotiations, and during our interview, she said, "If you're saying 'Yes' to something, that means you're saying 'No' to something." And that got me to thinking, as women of color, what sacrifices are we making to say yes to something? By saying yes to that underpaying job, what are we saying no to? I think about the times as an entrepreneur when I took unpaid speaking engagements for almost two years because I felt like I had to pay my dues and I didn't see my worth as a speaker. I still believe I have to pay my dues, but it doesn't mean I have to do everything for free. For those speaking gigs that I said yes to for no pay, what was I saying no to that might have resulted in compensation? I don't want to make it seem like everything is about money, because it's not, but we must have enough of it to take care of our responsibilities. What would have happened if after a year of unpaid speaking engagements, I started to negotiate an honorarium, or transportation, or recordings of myself so I could add these engagements to my speaking reel? I left a lot on the table, and I didn't put myself and my talents first. I hope you ask yourself this question the next time you negotiate for more money and, ultimately, your worth.

What About Your Friends?

Another part of closing this ridiculous wage gap is talking about our salaries with our friends and family. I would have never found out that doing the same work as my colleagues would result in each of us getting paid differently if we hadn't had conversations about salary. I feel like white people are better at this than women of color. White folks will tell you all their business, but people of color think that ain't none of your business. That is one thing I wish my girlfriends and I would do more of: talk about money. We discuss the money we make in vague terms. As black women, we are taught not to "tell all yo' business" and money is a big no-no. We don't talk about money when it's going good and we sure don't talk about it when it's going bad. We travel together and splurge at five-star restaurants, but no one has ever said how much they make.

Looking back at our conversations, I guess I just assumed everyone made at least six figures because of the way we all spent money. But when I think about it, that doesn't make sense. Some of us had to be using credit cards and spending beyond our means. We were able to talk about sex, relationships, and God knows what else—money should be in there too. Even though we all worked in different industries, I think salary conversations could have been helpful to each of us. And it would have been nice to know their salary negotiation stories and lessons learned or to have encouraged each other to ask for more if we weren't close to our financial goals. I only mention it because there is power in knowing. It hurts us when we don't know what other women are making. We can't change a game with made-up rules if we remain silent. And I am not saying, "Hey girl, go around and tell everyone what your take-home salary is," but let's start having more of these conversations as a way to encourage each other. You can at least give a range! Just think about it (smile).

I think getting accustomed to talking about our salaries is essential, and I decided to test my hypothesis out when a good friend came to New York City to visit me. I wanted to see if I could get us to drill into the money talk. We went to a fancy place I picked out in Tribeca (we are definitely black and bougie), and we started ordering like business as usual. We started talking about money, marriage, and credit scores—real fun adult dinner conversations (we are getting old!). She told me about a new guy she was serious about, and I asked her if they've discussed money. We laughed that you know it's serious when someone asks about your credit score and debt. It opened up a larger conversation about shame. Sometimes we are ashamed to let people behind the curtain of what's really going on with our finances. From there, we both were able to get vulnerable and talk about our debts and so on. It ended up being an organic, special conversation. I didn't have to whip out any "5 Ways to Talk about Money with Your Friend" lists—I allowed myself to be vulnerable, and she did too. If this is something that you want to try out, my main advice is to not make it weird!

Lastly, before I beat a dead horse. I am slightly thankful that white women started proclaiming they make X on a dollar, because that is when I woke the hell up and was like, *WHAT? You mean to tell me everyone isn't making the same?* It was an eye-opener for me, and had they not been highlighting what they make on a dollar, women of color wouldn't know we are getting a bum deal.

Black and Brown Coins Matter

As I mentioned before, negotiating our salaries and asking for more are not easy things to do. Ever since my corporate days, I have struggled with advocating for my worth. For entrepreneurs, pay isn't always so cut and dried, and I am always pushing myself to ensure I keep my bottom line first! As women of color we must continue to chip away at the wage gap until we reach parity, and that will take each of us advocating every chance we get because black and brown coins matter! "Listen, Linda," whether you work at the drive-through window at McDonald's or the top floor of Google, you deserve to be valued and paid accordingly, and like a nagging parent I'm going to remind you that this mentality starts with you owning your value. As someone who breathes and eats Beyoncé lyrics, I have had the pleasure of rewriting the song "Don't Hurt Yourself." It sums up the way that I pray women of color will look at their employers who are undervaluing them. Clears throat . . .

Who the—do you think I am,
you ain't working with no an average woman, boy,
you can watch my — twist, boy,
as I bounce to the next job, boy,
And keep your money, I'mma go get my own,
keep a bigger smile on my face, being alone,
God complex, getting underpaid, has motivated my ass,
call me by my correct first name, Innovator,
you will never recreate me, hell no.
When you underpay me, you underpay yourself!
Beyoncé be knowing!

Mic drop!

6

INVEST IN YO' SELF

I T NEVER GETS old watching Donna and Tom from *Parks and Recreation* tell us to "Treat yo' self." It is equally important to Invest in Yo' Self. As black and brown women, we have no problem spending hundreds of dollars on new hairdos, red-bottom shoes, and trips to Essence Fest, yet some wouldn't even consider spending the same amount of money on hiring an executive coach to help advance their career. I hate to break it to you, but if you invested in learning how to be a better negotiator or took a public speaking course, perhaps you would learn how to ask for more and have extra money to buy the hair you can't get in a bag at the local beauty supply store. No shade! Being your best advocate is not just dressing for the C-Suite but also making sure your skills match the shoes. How are you going to rock the latest fashions when your skills are stuck in 1999? What good is it to walk around the office in your new Yves Saint Laurent if you never get invited into the boardroom to show them off? What if instead you were in the boardroom giving them the fiercest shoe-a-cide game while delivering the presentation of a lifetime? Unfortunately, none of this happened because you never invested in fighting your fear of speaking in public. So you stayed in the same position, working on the same projects, with your new shoes. This is by no means a happy ending! Can you smell what the Rock is cooking? R-E-S-P-E-C-T in regard to your C-A-R-E-E-R requires an I-N-V-E-S-T-M-E-N-T, and college shouldn't be your last stop. We have to invest in our upward mobility. I don't think enough women of color invest in *their* professional development, myself included! Sometimes we think we've ascended to the top of the mountain and investing in our professional success is no longer required—but every step of our career will require enhanced skills; don't play yourself! There was a time in my career when I thought professional clothing was the only thing I needed to invest in; you know that old saying: "Dress for the role you want." I was missing out on the other part of that equation, which required me to level up in my skill set as well. One regret I have is never learning how to be more than "proficient" in Excel. At best, all I ever learned to do was bold, highlight, and delete. I noticed that certain colleagues were valued by many managers because they could make pivot tables and fancy charts. My level of Excel was as basic as they come, and I knew that and owned it. Funny thing is, Excel is still around a hundred years after I graduated from college, and my skills are pretty much the same. Even today, I sheepishly ask my cofounder Lauren, who is an Excel wizard, to do everything Excel-wise for our company because I never learned more than the basics. Excel has always been a pain point, and

I never took the time to invest in myself. Obviously, this is just one example. There were other skills that I identified and invested in, like public speaking. I was terrified to speak up in public, and I knew this fear would not help me get closer to my secured seat! What is that "Invest in Yo'Self" skill in your life that could be a huge benefit? It's up to you to figure out what that is! Maybe you should consider hiring a career coach or taking a webinar—that's a step in the right direction. There are many tools available to us if we want to level up, but we have to take advantage of those resources. Once I started investing in my professional development, my entire work game changed!

Some of you might be thinking, aw nah, hell naw, the only investment I made was my degree, and I'm still paying for that bad boy. First off, that is not the mindset to have when we think about the seat we want at the table. Why do you think women pay thousands of dollars to be part of mastermind groups? Or travel across the globe for retreats? They understand the cheat code; they know that in order to take it to the next level, something is required of them. It's called putting some skin in the game. Let's be clear: investing in yourself is not for your job, it's for you! So you can obtain everything you said you wanted out of your career when you started college or entered the workforce. Researching and utilizing additional career resources will help you advance in your career; you can't leave your professional development up to anyone else. You are your brand. You are an asset to yourself, and if you don't invest in the skills and training it takes to advance, your value will depreciate. And investing in yourself doesn't necessarily mean you use your own money; there might be scholarships or fellowships that allow you to invest in yourself. But the bottom line is . . . you have to take the initiative and take that first step! Cue Ciara's "Level Up."

Their Money

I know this investing-in-yourself thing might sound daunting and expensive, but did you know most companies have a professional development budget that you can tap into? It might not be publicized, but that doesn't mean your employer doesn't have, one. There are ways to leverage investing in yourself without using any of your coins; let's discuss what resources might be available via your employer. A professional development stipend or budget is money just sitting there available for you to enhance your skills! This money can be used for conferences, continuing education, and certifications. One year, I used my professional development stipend to attend the Black Enterprise Women of Power Summit. At this summit, I was able to meet other professional black women, and many of those women have turned into great friends that I added to my network. I've heard some of my peers use their stipends for anything from coaching certificates to professional subscriptions to their MBA's. As long as you can articulate how adding this new skill to your tool kit will benefit your team or the company's bottom line, you can get real creative with your professional development stipend.

Let's say one day you want to become a career coach. You could ask your employer if you could enroll in a coaching program because this new skill would help you become a stronger leader and serve as a mentor to your colleagues. Whatever your goal is, inquire about your company's professional development resources and how you can start using them today—don't wait. One of my former employers offered a professional development stipend, but I had to ask about it; no one ran up on me and told me about it. And not only did they offer a stipend, but also there were monthly lunch-and-learn classes that I could participate in. Attending those served two purposes: to network with new colleagues and to enhance my skill set. If your company or organization does not have a professional development program in place, think of this as a good opportunity to pitch creating the program. Creating a professional development program would allow you to take on a leadership role. Look at that—you kill two problems with one big idea! Additionally, some companies host free professional development resources that are open to the public. Often, I attend these types of events at Twitter and Microsoft, and I have never worked at either place!

I am not encouraging you to go broke by investing in yourself, but I am encouraging you to seek out the likely and unlikely resources for your development. Don't leave any potential opportunity on the table; this is your career we're talking about. Here is another way to look at it: what skills can you enhance today that will help position you for the next role? If you aspire to hold an executive title one day and you're currently just a few years into your career, what skills do you think someone in the C-Suite should have? Start to look at job descriptions for the roles you want, figure out what skills you need, and start investing in those skills. If someone offered you your dream job today, would you be ready to start tomorrow? Or would you have to say "no" because you weren't prepared skill wise to take on that role? Whose fault would that be? You have to assume the Lil' Kim mindset from the "Quiet Storm" remix, "I'm ten steps ahead of ya."

A Winner Needs a Coach

One untapped resource I discovered not being used by many women of color was career coaching. I wanted to understand why so many of us weren't investing in ourselves in this way, so I interviewed over one hundred women of color and asked them if they had ever used a career coach. Only five said yes. I asked them how they found out about executive coaching, and they said their white colleagues had one. So maybe you didn't even know this was a thing. And now that you know, you can start planning how to incorporate this resource to assist in furthering your career. "Listen, Linda," in the perfect workplace scenario your manager would sit down with you, map out a path for advancement, encourage you to take advantage of all the resources your company has to offer, and mention how career coaching helped him or her move into a management position. But we know that hardly ever happens. Most managers are not invested in your success, so you can't leave your professional development up to them. Most managers are just trying to make it through the day and check the boxes. For those women who are lucky enough to have a manager that gives a damn, God bless you both! Unfortunately, the reality is that if you don't have someone other than yourself invested in your career, then you must identify your blind spots and figure out where there's room to improve.

Career coaches can be used to help you negotiate, advocate, and plan the next step in your career. They provide their clients with a curated career road map. I have used my own resources to hire a coach on a couple of occasions based on the career "need" I had at that time. I last used a career coach in the summer of 2018 to enhance my leadership skills. I have to hold myself accountable to the people I lead—I take my position as CEO seriously! One of the tools that my coach, Aishah Hunter, used was called the Energy Leadership Assessment. *Forbes* named this assessment tool as one of the top eleven assessments every executive should take. During this assessment, I learned about the seven levels of leadership and how my energy shows up at each level. I was coached on how to level up in areas where I had room for improvement. The investment that I made during the time it took to take the assessment and the session with the coach not only helped me strengthen my leadership skills but also benefits those I work alongside.

Another coach I admire and respect is Tiffany Southerland, founder of Four Corners Coaching. I often recommend Tiffany's services to my friends because she knows what it's like to have a seat at someone else's table and to build your own. Her unique perspective helps many clarify their career goals. I spoke with Tiffany about the benefits of hiring a coach and her thoughts on the importance of women of color investing in this resource:

Women of color often carry the weight of taking care of other people, usually at the expense of our healing, goals, and development. This is just as true in our professional journeys as it is in our personal lives. We are taught to show up and work twice as hard. We are not always taught, though, that much more is required to advance. Coaching provides an excellent opportunity for women of color to prioritize their advancement. It is a powerful way to make time for yourself and invest in your vision for your career and life as a whole woman. Coaching gives a woman protected time that is dedicated to her goals, development, and advancement. By working with a coach, either one-on-one or in a group setting, women are given the opportunity to explore possibilities, be vulnerable, and be supported as they develop actionable strategies that will move them toward a self-determined version of their life and career.

I agree with Tiffany. Plus, I would never advise you to invest in a resource that I wouldn't invest in as well. Have you noticed that every professional athlete has a coach? Why would you be any different? You are the captain of your team. You are the point guard for every shot you shoot. And, you are the goalie that has to keep out lame managers that would try and stifle your career. You can't win this workplace game without a coach. Well, you could win without one, but wouldn't it be easier if you had one? Coaching can be expensive, but so can a cup of premium coffee each morning. We choose what we want to invest in. It's not lost on me that not everyone can afford a career coach. This is why we created Career Boot Camps at The Memo. We wanted to make career education and exposure accessible, whether you are a recent graduate, in transition, or making a six-figure salary. And remember, your employer might pay for professional development resources like career coaching, and you could also request professional development while negotiating your recruiting package or during your annual review. As I said before, leave no stone unturned when it comes to your professional development.

Proficiency Isn't Enough Anymore

Besides considering a career coach or investing in a similar career resource, it's important to think about developing your long-term skills. Remember that career blueprint I told you to think about? We'll get to that in more depth, but your long-term skills all relate to where you want to take your career. Investing in yourself will require adding new skills to keep you marketable. In this new economy, it's not enough to work for thirty to forty years and receive a gold watch when you retire. If something happens to your job before you get to retirement, you need to be marketable elsewhere. Recently, I was at a McDonald's, and the manager asked each person to place their orders at the self-serve kiosk because they were understaffed, instead of going up to the counter to order. When I left McDonald's, I couldn't help but think about the future of the workforce and the potential downsizing that could occur as a result of self-serve kiosks. Conversely, I thought about the opportunities that might present themselves for their employees and the career exposure to tech, which might ignite a passion to learn more about the technology behind the kiosk, which might result in a desire to learn a new skill in the tech field. There is nothing wrong with reinvesting in your skills, and we must be self-aware enough to realize when it's time to seek out new credentials or certifications. For example, if you have been a certified public accountant for the last thirty years, the ever-changing economic markets and technology would require you to stay up-to-date on the latest software and read up on how blockchain might affect the future of your industry. We no longer can skate by with our skills from the past and expect to remain competitive in the future. I don't want any of us to be afraid of growing older in the workplace or dismiss how ageism has forced talented people out of their careers. Ageism is a real thing, but perhaps taking additional professional development training to help underscore that you are still a viable part of the talent pool could be helpful in your next career transition. None of us are exempt from staying on top of the latest trends. Or if you're a recent grad with limited work experience, how do you describe the leadership roles you held that helped you prepare for the position you want to apply for today? Don't let your age stop you from investing in yourself.

We all need the extra investment to help us succeed. Here's another way to look at it: I remember when I put together my first résumé. Back then it was trendy to put how many words per minute you could type. In high school, I was required to take a typing course (LORDT, I am showing my age). If I prepared my résumé today with those same words per minute as a skill set, they would throw my résumé in the trash and think my skills were outdated. Or if you are still putting "proficient in Microsoft" on your résumé, honey, they are throwing that résumé in the trash too. Any person with a computer and Internet is proficient in Microsoft Office. You might not be aware of or up to speed on the latest skills and trends in the workplace, and I know résumés might seem like a petty thing to focus on, but if you don't know what they look like in the twenty-first century or if you haven't worked in a decade or more, you can't afford to not invest in yourself. And if you aren't sure what a more modern résumé looks like or you want to transition into using a virtual résumé or create a personal website, you should connect with a career coach or even a trusted friend who can help you.

Recently, I offered to help one of my relatives update her résumé. She had been out of the traditional workforce for decades and found herself needing to return to work. For months she was sending out résumés and receiving no bites. I could sense her frustration, and since I am in the career development field, I wanted to be of service. I am pretty sure she didn't have the most up-to-date résumé and was using her work experience from the 1970s and 1980s to tell her career story. She refused my help and was in denial about the need to level up. It hurts me to say this, but she still hasn't been called in for an interview. Often we want others to invest in us when there's an investment we must first make in ourselves. We cannot afford to be ambivalent about our careers at any age.

Mindset

Another important aspect of investing in yourself is creating a new mindset. In the next chapter, I will delve deeper into how you build a healthy mindset on the road to securing your seat, but here I will touch on it a bit in regard to our personal commitment to and investment in ourselves. I love watching interviews of Serena Williams, who makes no apology for investing in her career and her desire for total domination. She never shies away from that narrative. She doesn't assume her competitors or coaches know that she is playing to win; she makes it very clear that winning is her goal. When Serena returned from maternity leave, she did an interview at Wimbledon in which she said, "It's what makes me great. I always have to play everyone at their greatest, so I have to be greater." We should all take a page or two from the playbook of one of the greatest athletes of all time.

Serena has never been afraid to be vocal. She invests in herself by being her best advocate. How are you advocating for yourself? If you think you are the greatest at what you do and want more from your employer or career, then it's up to you to shout it from the rooftops. You can't assume your manager or the executive team knows what you want out of *your* career; they are not mind readers, and they have other employees to manage as well. It's unrealistic to think they are planning your future promotion when you have never vocalized wanting more. Now, don't get me wrong, some groups of people don't have to do anything and they will still get promoted over the black or brown women who have busted their butts for the last ten years. But speaking up is an important investment, regardless of the outcome. And, I get it, I get it, as women we often have a hard time highlighting our achievements and advocating for ourselves; this soft muscle is not one that many of us feel comfortable flexing. Remember when I said you have to invest in yo' self? Well, this is part of that investment, baby girl. Time to level up and Harlem shake through your nerves.

If you want your employer to invest in your success, then *you* have to vocalize your wants! You must take the first step by believing you deserve what you asked for. In the book *Sister Love: The Letters of Audre Lorde and Pat Parker, 1974–1989* (edited by Julie Enszer with an intro by Mecca Jamilah

Sullivan), Audre Lorde wrote in a letter dated December 6, 1985: "Beware feeling you're not good enough to deserve it and beware feeling you're too good to need it." In other words, you owe this act of investing in yourself, to yourself! It's not easy, but I promise the investment will always be worth it.

You're probably starting to ask yourself two questions: (1) What do I want? and (2) How will I ever articulate my wants and desires to my manager or team? One way to figure out how you want your employer to invest in you and what you want your legacy at work to look like is to create a purpose statement.

I found it quite helpful many years ago to produce a purpose statement for my career. This works in conjunction with your blueprint to help steer your decisions and investments (of time and money). Before you can create your career blueprint, you must start with your purpose! Recently, I started revising my career purpose statement to help me decipher whether I am spending my time on projects that embody my purpose. For example, my career purpose statement is: *I want to help catalyze equity for women of color in the workplace.* I have to continuously ask myself if the things I am saying yes to align with my career purpose statement. I suggest taking time out to think through your career goals and what's important to you as you continue to secure your seat at the table. When I first wrote out my career purpose statement, it was about two hundred words long. Over time I was able to refine it to a simple yet impactful statement. The sooner you can narrow in on what you want and need out of your career, the easier it will be when you look for a new job or articulate to your current manager how you would like them to partner with you on your career path. For those who might need a little help crafting their career purpose statement, use the following sentence to help you get started.

My career purpose is —————— and when I look back on my career, I hope I can say —————— . The turning point in my career was —————— and I realized that I had the power to re-create my narrative. My values are —————— .

I mentioned that you need to get real clear on your personal career needs to help you create a career blueprint. I would encourage you to think about Maslow's Hierarchy of Needs; he says we have basic, psychological, and self-fulfillment needs. Now take that same framework and place your needs in a career context. Start to think through how you want your career to work for you. For example: your current job might not pay enough. Therefore, it's hard for you to pay your rent and buy groceries—you are living paycheck to paycheck. Your job is not meeting your basic needs. How do you find a job that does? You first have to decide what your basic needs are and build from there. You can start to build out the skeleton of your career blueprint by identifying each of your workplace needs. Ask yourself some of the following questions to help you dig deeper into where you want your career to take you.

1. Your Needs. What do you need from your career?

2. Your Happiness. What type of work do you most enjoy?

3. Your Why. Why do you want this change, and how will it enhance your career?

4. Your Timeline. How long will it take you to execute your plans?

By getting clear on your career needs by answering these questions, you will be able to create a career blueprint. Your needs might change as you climb the ladder, and that's okay too. In addition to your career hierarchy of needs, I would recommend creating a career blueprint statement you can refer back to from time to time, to help you stay on the path to your career goals. Now let's build on your career needs to get even closer to creating your career blueprint:

My short-term career goals are _____. My long-term career goals are _____. And my hope is to leave an impact in the following ways _____.

These sample statements are meant to help you get started and to serve as a reference to help you gain clarity on your career blueprint and the ways in which you can start investing in yourself!

Once you have a working document of your career purpose statement and your career blueprint, continue to work on it, remembering that it's a work in progress. At the very least, it will help you articulate how you need your company to invest in your success. It will help guide your future conversations about your career.

Sharing Your Blueprint

Let's quickly address how to start conversations with your manager or "the powers that be" about your career blueprint. Your manager is your main point of contact; you should already be having regular one-on-one meetings. If you aren't having those, then start by requesting one—maybe weekly or biweekly. During these meetings, you can address your desire for advancement and share appropriate parts of your career purpose statement. Don't be ambivalent about what you want. Be clear. Ask your manager if you can discuss a roadmap for advancement. In this moment you will find out whether this is a place that will foster your growth or whether you have a good-for-nothing manager. Wouldn't you rather know now if you will have opportunities to advance, or nah?

Sometimes these conversations will surprise you and open up amazing opportunities, and other times they can serve as a reality check. You might never get the opportunity to advance in your current position, and investing in yourself to get the hell out of there is your next strategic move. You need to know either way. You won't regret being intentional, strategic, and prepared in articulating to senior management your desire to move up the ladder. Go back to Chapter 2, "Building Your Squad." I discuss how I made a key connection with one senior leader that helped launch my career. All you need is one! Lastly, in Drake's song, "Underground Kings," he sings, "I'm the greatest man / I said that before I knew I was." In that same song, he also says, "I was pushing myself to get something that I deserved." Also, the great fighter Muhammad Ali was one of the best self-talk people on the planet. He was constantly advocating for himself and had a strong sense of belief in his skill set. He once said, "I'm not the greatest. I'm the double greatest. Not only do I knock 'em out, I pick the round. I'm the boldest, the prettiest, the most superior, most scientific, most skillfullest fighter in the ring today." We have to have that same energy about ourselves! Like the young kids say, "Keep that same energy!" If you don't advocate for yourself, who will? And self-advocacy is a worthwhile investment.

Own Your Narrative

Investing in yourself, as you can see, includes developing both soft skills—like communication—and hard skills—like Excel. You can't advance unless you have both. Once you have learned to be your best advocate, it's time to own your narrative. Storytelling is one of the most powerful tools you can have in your tool kit. Investing in learning how to tell your career story is essential. As women of color, we often feel like we have to hide our ambition. Stop that! We are high achievers and want more out of our careers, and that is okay—don't hide it! Never dim your light in order to make someone else feel comfortable. And never, ever allow anyone to write your career narrative. You are the alpha and omega of your own career! For example, you might be a new mom, but you can still be considered for a job overseas. Or maybe you are single, but that doesn't mean your employer can work you like a dog because they think you have nothing else going on. Oh, and perhaps you are attractive, and they think you might be a distraction, so they don't place you on specific projects with their male clients. Hear me loud and clear: Articulate your desire to advance and own your past experience. Don't let other people's biases and stupidity stop your show. It starts with you. You are your best advocate. No matter what you do, don't leave your career advancement in the hands of someone else. If you do, they will keep you in the same basic-ass box they put other women in. This is a huge part of investing in yourself. In other words, if you're dating the person of your dreams and you know you want to get married, but you're afraid to bring it up because this information might run them off—so you just go with the flow. And all the while you're frustrated and wondering where things stand. Don't treat your career like a mediocre relationship. Never be afraid to want more in your job or anything that pertains to your happiness.

Career Tool Kit

I firmly believe that we all need a career tool kit, just as some women keep an extra hand sanitizer or lipstick in their purse—just in case. This tool kit is the way we act on our purpose statement, act on our blueprint. We should adopt the same mentality when it comes to our careers. We should be ready, just in case! Don't give anyone a reason to tell you "no" because you weren't prepared. What's in your tool kit? We all have different skill sets and are in various stages of our careers, but there are some standard tools (like hammers, screwdrivers, or scissors) that we all need to keep handy in the event we need them. As we continue the conversation about investing in ourselves, think about what areas in your career need enhancing or which "tools" are missing from your career tool kit. Start with a basic exercise of exploring your strengths and weaknesses. This skills assessment could be as simple as a list in two columns. In one column make a list of the hard and soft skills that you consider to be career assets, and in the second column, make a list of the hard and soft skills that might not win you awards just yet! How does the list of skills that you want to improve align with your career purpose statement? As you can see, in this chapter we are building out your career blueprint so you know how you want to invest in having a more fulfilling career.

Start with choosing two skills from the second column that you want to invest in to make your career tool kit stronger. For example, public speaking was in my column two. Catalyzing equity for women of color at work requires me to advocate, which means speaking on behalf of other women of color who might not have the space to speak up for themselves (yet). So it makes sense to invest in making myself more comfortable speaking in public. Additionally, public speaking is one of the two standard tools that have been helpful at every stage of my career (networking is the other). When I feel like I need a refresher, I invest in the most updated versions of my career tools. I never assume I don't need to re-up!

Let me make a quick side note on those two critical tools for me, public speaking and networking: There will never be a time in your career when you don't have to speak in public. I'm not saying you have to go on a world tour and conduct motivational speeches, but having a seat at the table requires you to use your voice. I used to be deathly afraid of speaking up in meetings. I felt that what I had to say didn't matter or someone might think it was stupid. What I quickly learned was that those who spoke up seemed to (1) get heard and (2) gain access to the table at some point in time. I decided this was a skill I needed to work on because what I have to contribute is important. My interest in being a more effective speaker was bigger than my fear of speaking, so I went for it. I began to take public speaking courses and to force myself to speak up in meetings when appropriate. I even volunteered during projects to be the person that presents the group's findings. Because there aren't enough women of color inside most companies, we can't afford to stay silent and let others speak on our behalf. Start small and before you know it, you will be speaking up more and more. Again, public speaking is not something I did for my employer; I invested in this tool for myself. By assessing my skills, I learned to identify my strengths and weaknesses and leverage them for my tool kit. Public speaking was one of my biggest strengths that I never knew I had. Now I get paid to come and speak, and when you turn a weakness into a strength, that is powerful!

Relationship building was also something I saw as a strength of mine. The part I didn't enjoy was networking. Working as a consultant and philanthropic advisor forced me to be a people person. Networking is a critical tool. It's hard to advance if you aren't cultivating new and existing relationships. I can just imagine that some of you want to skip to the next chapter when I mention networking. But networking doesn't have to be daunting; building new connections can be fun. Introverts or extroverts, we all need a healthy network we can rely on. Start small, and it can be as simple as speaking to new people in the office, joining a professional organization, or attending a Meetup group. Most of my career I traveled a lot, and it required me to work in different states and client sites. Essentially, I could have new colleagues every few months. I used those opportunities to build relationships with everyone, from the janitor to the CEO. I learned that every position has value. Some of the interns who worked for me over a decade ago, I treated like colleagues. Hell, I knew one day they might be my boss—ha ha, but I think you get my point. If you want to advance within your current company, you will be required to take some initiative and build out your workplace alliances (think back to Chapter 2, when I talked about how to build your squad). The more people who know you and can vouch for you inside the workplace, the better. But this only happens when you network. People can't advocate for you if they don't know anything about you. And I will let you in on a little insider tip. I used to hate going to networking events or work birthday parties because I felt like they were awkward, forced interactions. Before I would head over to the shindig, I would play the 1990s Jodeci song, "Come and Talk to Me": "Come and talk to me, / I really want to meet you. / I really want to know you." It would make me laugh and put me in the mindset to make networking fun. Hey, don't judge me, you got something better to offer?

You're Worth It

As you build your career you will add more tools, and before you know it, you will have a toolbox full of what you need, when you need it. Investing in yo' self isn't something just for those starting out in their careers; it's for every woman who wants to advance. But it will require you to be self-aware. Maybe you don't need any of the tools mentioned in this chapter, but I guarantee if you don't level up and invest in enhanced skills, you're blocking future career opportunities. I had the pleasure of facilitating a workshop at the Urban League of Eastern Massachusetts, and the topic was bridging the digital divide for women of color. Most of the attendees were over forty-five years old, they understood that in a few years almost every job will have a technology component, and they didn't want to be left behind. In the workshop we discussed what new skills they should obtain that would allow them to stay active in the work-force, how being multidimensional is important, and the value of finding a safe space that allows them to be vulnerable about a transitional workforce. At the time of the workshop only 4.8 percent of black women were in tech roles. I explained that investing in new skills like user experience (UX) design would be beneficial in the tech world. There were also some misconceptions around every tech role requiring a computer science degree. They were elated to learn of the many nontechnical roles they could apply for in the tech industry. For example, tech companies need accountants too. The takeaway for them was they didn't have to be afraid to invest in new skills; those skills will position them for upward mobility.

You can use your career purpose statement and short- and long-term career goals to help you build the tool kit to achieve your blueprint and secure your seat at your table. You don't want to be stuck with old skool skills moving into the new jack swing. Or better yet, you don't want to be doing the running man, while everyone else is milly rocking. Take it from Beyoncé, she levels up for every tour and every album. Get your sh— together and level up by investing in yo' self!

7

EMPIRE STATE OF MIND

THE DAY THAT Kanye West started talking about en-slaved people having a choice to be oppressed for over four hundred years, I was reminded that the mind is a terrible thing to waste. In addition, self-deprecation is one of the most dangerous ways to deconstruct our mindset and self-worth. And equally as dangerous as Kanye's so-called free thinking against my ancestors is when we talk ourselves out of a potential career opportunity or tell ourselves we aren't worthy and don't belong. If we think we don't deserve the best career or the highest salary, we will never obtain a career highlight reel we can reflect back on with a smile. Winning requires us to toss out a piss-poor mindset. Self-worth is another word for self-esteem. If we don't put value on our own worth, then we leave it up to other people to help define it for us. Do you remember the first time you heard the Jay-Z and Alicia Keys song "Empire State of Mind" and how it made you feel? You went from zero to one hundred real quick, and those lyrics made you feel like you could conquer the world! You could have been living in rural Mississippi, and you still felt like the world was yours; you didn't need to be in New York City. To thrive in the workplace as a woman of color, you need an Empire State of Mind, even when the environment will have you feeling like adopting an Enemy State of Mind. It takes acquiring an Empire State of Mind to push through the BS that is already embedded in most workplace cultures. Women of color must adopt a strong mindset so that we can't be swayed from reaching our desired positions, even if the playing field isn't level. Adopting an "I can make it anywhere" mindset will keep you standing strong on the days you feel like running out the door in tears. For so long we have learned to function in a dysfunctional work environment, and it will take an intentional shift in our thinking to replace self-doubt, insecurities, self-criticism, and other negative thoughts.

Impostor Syndrome

Imposter syndrome has become everyone's favorite buzzword. Hell, every Ivy League graduate now enters the room claiming to deal with imposter syndrome. For years communities of color have felt this way, yet we didn't have some fancy white word to call it. Let me tell you what "the syndrome" is really like for women of color. Growing up, my family struggled financially. Being the oldest child and seeing my parents struggle always worried me. It worried me so much, I've been working since I was twelve years old. I started out babysitting, delivering phone books (when phone books were lit), and delivering newspapers. Our family struggles affected the field trips we could go on, the school clothes we could buy, the places we could afford to stay, and the free lunch programs we qualified for. Those experiences shaped my young and impressionable mind. I always had the mindset that I didn't want to struggle that way when I became an adult. For better or worse, those struggles shaped the driven career woman I became. I was obsessed with working so hard and achieving everything that many people might deem as successful, or at least what I thought equaled success. And when you grow up financially challenged, a couple of things follow you into adulthood: you never forget where you came from, and you work harder because you fear you might end up reliving the same experience as an adult. The blessing and the curse of my obsession with success was that on paper I was achieving success, but mentally, I was always worried about what others thought, wanting desperately to prove I was not a product of my environment, and spending a lot of unnecessary energy trying to keep up with the Joneses. But I was never comfortable in my own skin, and I was grateful for every opportunity that came my way, as if I hadn't worked my butt off for it.

When I entered into the workforce I realized that many of my colleagues came from privileged backgrounds. And their tone-deaf nature allowed them to assume everyone else must have had the same experiences. My already shaky mindset then led to feelings of inadequacy. I didn't want these white people to know I came from humble beginnings. And Drake hadn't yet made it popular to start out from the bottom. I wanted them to think I belonged in their club. Some might call it assimilation. Would they accept me if they knew that my family had to use food stamps (I didn't want them feeling sorry for me), that I'm bad at math because we couldn't afford one of those fancy-ass Texas Instrument calculators, or that I went to a community college because I didn't have access to the same resources they did? I was constantly questioning my worth. I never vocalized it, but it was slowly killing me inside. I started to equate their privilege with my lack of privilege, and it got the best of me. What would they think if I told them I can't remember how many apartments or houses I've lived in because we moved so much, while they rattle on about going back to their childhood homes for the holidays or their second home in Aspen. I managed to become the colleague who was everyone's friend, and I gave just enough of myself to have good working relationships. But I refused to talk about my past. My working environment made me feel that I had to prove to them I knew which fork to use at the dinner table. I would closely study which fork they would pick up; my best china was the paper product brand Chinet, and I used plastic cutlery. I always felt like I had something to prove, like eating sushi and caviar for the first time. I was secretly drowning in my feelings and being one of the only ones doesn't always allow space to be vulnerable, nor did I have anyone at home that understood the two worlds I was trying to balance. My so-called woes just made it easier for family and friends to call me bougie. The best way to describe it was that one minute I felt like Superman due to what I had accomplished, and the next I would retreat to Clark Kent and just put on my glasses. The "syndrome" I was experiencing is called insecurity. And this insecurity led to a constant feeling of anxiety.

See, I worked hard to get in those rooms, but once I got there I questioned everything that got me there. I didn't feel the inclusion, which started to slowly erode my feeling of belonging. I fought so hard to become that I was losing myself at what I was *being*. On the outside I appeared confident and put together, but if you pulled back the curtain, I still saw myself as that little black girl with a book of food stamps hoping none of the kids at school would see me and label me "the poor kid." This is some debilitating stuff! I had my hang-ups about my past, and now I was thrust into a world of white tablecloths, seven-course meals, and country clubs. These people go on legit vacations to Thailand and Europe. At that time, I didn't even have a passport. As a kid, I was happy when we were able to drive two hours away and swim in the Residence Inn pool— that was a vacation to me. A memory that I held dear somehow had me feeling ashamed. I felt I had to hide who I was. And all of this made me question whether I should be at the table. Am I here because I worked hard for this, or because they are trying to fill a quota?

Toni Morrison said it best, "If you want to fly, you have to give up the sh— that weighs you down." I came to my fork in the road, a Bone Thugs-n-Harmony kinda crossroads, and I knew if I was going to continue to advance my career and be impactful, I needed to deal with my mental crap. It wasn't about my colleagues or the way I grew up; it was all about me and how I saw myself. I wanted to blame the white people at my job who told me I needed to eat couscous (which I found out I was allergic to) and my low-income background but not everything I was projecting onto my situation. I controlled this narrative in my head. Yes, they were tone-deaf and privileged, but I was dealing with issues that had nothing to do with them and everything to do with me. It wasn't clear to me at first, but I was battling low self-esteem. I had to change my way of thinking and work on my insecurities. The road to the table is not created equal, but once you secure your seat, how every-one got there shouldn't mean as much—it's what you do with your seat once you sit down that matters. And since women of color already have systemic battles at work to face, we can't afford to let our mental state become our own worst enemy.

I was in my head too much and if I'm being honest, I was just happy to be in the room, happy to have a place at the ta-ble. For a long time I didn't even speak up; I just went with the status quo. As the only black woman in the room, I was scared I might get put out. Let's keep it 100 percent real: there was a time when there were none in the room and these people thought that sh— was okay. I was too stuck on stupid to un-derstand that I needed to rebuild my mindset so I could shape the foundation of the room and bring other women of color with me. I was scared that at any moment I would be told to go. I couldn't call Ghostbusters with my issues, so I decided I needed a therapist to unpack everything I was thinking and feeling. Our forever first lady Michelle Obama was spot on when she stated at the United States of Women Summit in Los Angeles in 2018, "So many of us have gotten ourselves at the table, but we're still too grateful to be at the table to really shake it up." So we sit down, be quiet, and do what we're told. We aren't familiar with any other working environments, so sometimes we are unaware of how much power we possess. Looking back, it makes me sick to think I sat in countless meetings and did not say one word! I wish I had known Mrs. Obama in the early 2000s. This was the advice I needed to hear as a young, professional, black woman. Selah!

The Road to Recovery

In order to get closer to my intended Empire State of Mind and truly believe that I was more than a conqueror, I had to stop centering my story around my deficit and focus on my future assets. As some of you might know, going to a therapist was frowned upon in the black community until not too long ago. We go to two places when we are dealing with troubled waters: on our knees for prayer or to the pastor at church. Both of those places have served me well, but I needed to speak to someone who didn't know me and who could be objective. Not to mention that therapy would be paid for through my health insurance—far be it from me to waste all that good money I pay each month to have this insurance. I didn't know what the therapist would end up telling me or if she thought I needed pills; I just knew I needed an Iyanla Vanzant to help fix my life. This is a hard thing for me to admit. I am one of those people that hold my feelings in and eventually, I *might* talk about what is bothering me, but that is not a go-to button for me. Being the oldest of three kids, I took on the role as the tough one, the helper, the one everyone could depend on. I felt like going to see a therapist was a sign of weakness—why did I need to talk it out with a stranger? Again, at the time, therapy was not something the black community was encouraging, and I felt like I was letting God down because I wasn't taking this matter to the church. Let me stop and remind each person reading this book: there is nothing wrong with therapy, and there is nothing wrong with you. I wish someone would have told me that, because I had all these hang-ups and I didn't feel good about myself when I made the decision. I believed the lie!

Therapy is not a sign of weakness; it's a sign that you want to live a healthier and happier life. Oddly enough, after going to therapy for three years, I found out that what I initially thought was causing all my insecurities ('cause you know we love to self-diagnose) wasn't quite right. I uncovered some underlying issues. I needed to take ownership of my thoughts and start to own the woman I wanted to be, not base that on anyone else's narrative. Growing up with government cheese in my refrigerator turned out to be not the problem, but part of the symptom. But that, my friends, is an entirely different book. What my therapist helped me unpack is that I needed a new way of thinking and seeing myself. I had to look Minda in the mirror and ask her to change her ways. I needed that Empire State of Mind that I mentioned. If I made it this far, against all the odds, I could make it anywhere, and that includes being the only black woman in the room with people who see nothing wrong with this power structure. I had to stop feeding my insecurity monster, or I was going to continue to be my worst enemy. I looked back on what got me to this point: the hard work and the sleepless nights. Packing up my apartment and moving across the country for an opportunity I wasn't sure would work out. I was obsessed with "making it," and I was also obsessed with whether "they" would accept me or not. I put too much value on how other people perceived me. I might not have gone to the best schools in the country or had a trust fund set up, but darn it, I belonged every bit as much as everyone else did. And I used to believe that, but somewhere along the way, I lost it. But, I had enough sense to know I needed to find it again. Even Justice Sonia Sotomayor said she experienced imposter syndrome, "I have spent my years since Princeton, while at law school and in my various professional jobs, not feeling completely a part of the worlds I inhabit. I am always looking over my shoulder wondering if I measure up." And just like Justice Sotomayor, I didn't want to spend my best years questioning if I measured up; my frame of mind was more important than any seat at the table. Securing my Empire State of Mind and a seat at the table would allow me to be *unstoppable!*

I valued the money I was making and the title changes, but in the back of my head I was dealing with a syndrome that a prescription couldn't fill. I had to fill myself back up with positive affirmations and self-love. You can prepare yourself externally with school, conferences, and all the workshops money can buy, but at the beginning and the end of the day, is your spirit right? As Lauryn Hill sings in "Doo Wop": "How you gon' win when you ain't right within—Come again?" I honestly don't think I could have started The Memo if I hadn't done this internal, emotional work. Once I was able to understand my responsibility and accountability in holding a position that could influence change, I had to know without a shadow of a doubt that my voice mattered and I didn't owe these white people anything—I owed more to myself. I had to be strong enough to use my power, and now my privilege, to create space for other women of color.

Kendrick Lamar put it this way, "I got loyalty, royalty inside my DNA." And thank God, I was able to believe that for myself—despite the lack of racial diversity in leadership. Changing my mindset didn't happen overnight, just because I read a couple of quotes. I had to make the conscious decision to adopt a positive and healthy approach to thrive in a workplace that isn't always thinking about how to include me. I was done just surviving! I had done as much "fake it until you make it" as I could, and it was killing me softly. There's a famous quote that I have heard many versions of. It originated with James Crook, but I am going to Minda-ize it: A woman who wants to lead must first turn her back on the crowd. I cared too much what the crowd might think of me. I had to turn my back on them and work on me. In addition to making sure I was right within, of course; I prayed and attended church—that is part of my life—but also I started going to yoga and adopted mindful meditation practices. And for the skeptics, I am not in a cult: all these things are essential to obtaining a healthy state of mind.

Self-care isn't just massages and binging on your favorite episodes of *Billions*. And let's be clear, I am not preaching that you need a therapist and a ten-day yoga retreat in the Bahamas. What I am advocating is making your mindset a priority. If you aren't yet in the room, let alone at the table, then preparing for the highs and lows that require you to be mentally fit. You must explore what that looks like for you, but I encourage you not to ignore your internal needs while striving for the external ones. Even to this day, I still have to do temperature checks with myself to make sure I recognize the triggers that might make me question my position as I ascend in my career. I felt the "syndrome" trying to pop its ugly head back up when I started my business and when I closed my first book deal. I had to remind myself, *Aye, Minda, this is what you worked hard for, this is what you prayed for; stop tripping and let's live limitlessly and reap the fruits of the people who paved the path before you and your investment to get here!*

Noninclusive Workplace Cultures

I shared how I had to prepare for my Empire State of Mind to enter and remain sane in the workplace, yet this doesn't take away the systemic layers embedded into a workplace culture that also play a huge role in how we see ourselves. One of my grandmothers grew up in an orphanage in England, and she was the only brown child in the orphanage. She was a product of an interracial relationship, and in the 1940s she was looked at as an outcast. Even though all the young girls at the orphanage were in a similar situation, none of the staff at the orphanage made an effort to try and make her feel included; she was continuously reminded by their actions and words that she was different. She never felt like she belonged, and she battled that feeling her entire life. She spent the rest of her life chasing a feeling of being included. You can only imagine how that shaped how she learned to show up in the world. I share this story because the workplace has set up a similar power structure.

Representation isn't some charitable act; it's an intentional action that has the power to shape our mindsets and even the thinking of generations. So when you hear someone say, "Representation matters," it matters to those who are never represented, and being represented and seen has the power to change the way women of color view themselves and the positions we aspire to. Over the years we have read countless articles and essays on the lack of representation in the workplace as it pertains to women of color, especially in leadership and executive roles. When every statistic in the book shows the lack of investment in black and brown women by corporate America and nonprofit organizations, it confirms that we are not making any of these inequalities up, because the numbers don't lie. In fact, women of color endure a lot in the workplace: we do not have the privilege of representation, and we have to continually battle doubt about whether we belong, because we don't see many of us in leadership positions. I will tell you from personal experience that it's hard to be what you can't see. It's hard to keep leaning in when you sit in a workplace for years and never see open positions filled with other people of color. And it's extremely hard to constantly hear your leadership talk about diversity and inclusion and take no real steps toward hiring and retaining diverse talent. How are we supposed to give you our best work and stay positive when we are constantly met with this insensitivity from our leaders? I don't even have the vocabulary to articulate the frustration! To be completely honest, I feel the same sentiment Serena Williams felt at the 2018 US Open when she told Carlos Ramos, "You owe me an apology!" Companies and organizations owe women of color several apologies! This particular workplace issue has nothing to do with us, but everything to do with a lack of intentionality on the part of corporate America. And even with that being the truest thing I have ever written, women of color still have to remain vigilant and not allow these systemic layers to hinder our Empire State of Mind. There are future generations of women of color counting on us to finish this race and make it better when they arrive! Please don't bite the apple and leave the garden before your time. Develop mental toughness to stay on your path.

The military coined the phrase "moral injury." According to the National Center for Posttraumatic Stress Disorder, veterans experience moral injury, and it's defined as "Psychological trauma or moral injury is a construct that describes extreme and unprecedented life experience including the harmful aftermath of exposure to such events. Events are considered morally injurious if they transgress deeply held moral beliefs and expectations. Rooted in religious or spiritual beliefs, or culture-based, organizational, and group-based rules about fairness, the value of life, and so forth." In other words, the sometimes harsh working environments that veterans are subject to create trauma; we could also make a similar argument for women of color and the trauma we face in the workplace. For example, women of color face experiences in the workplace that could be viewed as "harmful events" that might lead to bouts of posttraumatic stress disorder. I find it interesting that the National Center for PTSD says the side effects are shame, guilt, anxiety, and anger. By no means am I certified to diagnose any of us, but some of the same side effects lead me to believe many women of color might relate to feelings of moral injury as we build our careers. (For the record, I am not disrespecting our veterans. I have the utmost respect for their sacrifices for our country. My father is a veteran.) But when I think about moral injury in the context of women of color in the workplace, the feelings of shame, guilt, anxiety, and anger are all too real!

Many of our work environments are not providing us our shot at the pursuit of happiness—they restrict us from advancing in our careers. I think many white CEOs should go back and reread this portion of Dr. Martin Luther King Jr.'s "I Have a Dream" speech: "I have a dream that my four little children will one day live in a nation where they will not be judged by the color of their skin but by the content of their character." Women of color have to wake up every morning and be judged by the color of our skin, and some might push back and say our lack of advancement has nothing to do with race. Well, then, someone please explain to me why black and brown women are well educated but lack opportunities to advance in leadership roles while white men and women have these opportunities?

Despite this injury, we get up morning after morning and continue to serve from a place of sacrifice and disappointment—often knowing that no matter how hard we lean in, we might never reach that table. And sometimes we bring this moral injury of horrible workplace experiences, ill-willed colleagues, and lack of ascension with us each day when we arrive at the office. Some of us even bring this moral injury from our last jobs to our current and future ones, and we are so injured that we can't enjoy our future workplace wins. Erykah Badu told us black and brown girls to "pack light," but that's hard to do when your experiences tear you down rather than build you up! Can you fathom how much shame and anger we must suppress when we are seen as invisible at work? Not in a Marvel comic kind of way—this is straight-up dismissive. In order to thrive at work, we have to be mentally prepared for warfare, and take the advice Ms. Badu gave us in that song if we want to build our mindset: (1) "One day all them bags gon' get in your way" and (2) "You can't hurry up, 'cause you got too much stuff." Essentially, we can't let past or current workplaces stop us from going where we want to go. Pack light!

The Invisible Perfection Pressure

For a long time, I felt I had to be perfect. If I wanted to move up the ladder, I had to be at least ten times better than white men or women. Growing up black, we have always been taught that we don't have the luxury of slacking off or doing what the "white kids" do, because the rules are not set up the same. And those rules continue to play out for us as adults in the workplace. As women of color we have this extra glass ceiling, an extra layer of pressure to be perfect, that non–women of color will never have to crack, and I like to call this "invisible perfection pressure." When you ask white people what it takes to climb the corporate ladder, they always respond with some generic statement, "Work hard, and the sky's the limit!" We continue to work "harder" under a set of invisible rules with no playbook, and the expectation that we have to work so hard they can't deny us a seat adds this extra layer of pressure. Our hard work may not pay off. All women of color have ever known is hard work and resilience, so I am not sure how much harder we can work. We are under ridiculous amounts of pressure to check all of their boxes, and we still get overlooked for promotions. We seek to be equal participants in creating a better workplace culture, yet no matter how hard we work, white workplace norms continue to exist. Women of color are constantly expected to survive in a dual workplace mode: performing our job function to perfection while trying to demonstrate to white people our valuable contributions that would allow for more meaningful roles. We have the added pressure of trying not to make any mistakes while our counterparts are given a pass to be mediocre and often rewarded for their imperfections.

There was one promotion that I just knew was mine. I had the tenure and the credibility. I was already doing many of the functions. My entire team thought for sure that when our boss left, I would be promoted into her position. She was grooming me. Instead they put a white woman with less experience and a bad management track record in the position. She was nice enough, but she sure as hell wasn't better than me. For two years, I did just what I needed to do to get by. I was hurt, mad, and a bit disenchanted. I had given so many years of my career to this place, and this was the thanks I received. I had done everything that was required of me and then some—holding myself to a standard of perfection—and it still left me empty-handed. I am sure I am not the only person who has experienced this. Finally, they had their opportunity to add a black woman to the executive team, and instead they kept it 99.9 percent white. It's hard to maintain your Empire State of Mind when you are constantly reminded that no matter how good you might be, "they" just don't see or consider you for advancement. I won't lie and tell you I didn't want to give up.

Every day I wanted to quit under her leadership; it was hard to keep pushing forward. When we lean in, we never know the outcome. And it takes a strong mindset not to let the way white people have historically done business keep us from our corner office. I couldn't let their poor leadership record stop my career goals. Sometimes I wonder if non–people of color, those without disabilities, or those who don't identify as queer realize how emotionally draining it is to work forty hours or more per week for companies and organizations that don't actively try to advance them. Or when racial diversity does become a talking point, we are often presented with the lane excuse, "We aren't there yet." Experiencing this invisible perfection pressure day in and day out will make anyone question themselves. Again, these rules cannot be found in any human resource manual. And I believe we have to start calling these invisible perfection pressures out, or they will continue to be imposed on the next generation of women of color. And don't get me wrong, sis, these unwritten pressures to be perfect are hard to deal with, but we have worked too hard to turn back now. Resist, resist, resist the urge to give up on your career goals because of this invisible pressure. But also remember, you have the ability to chart a new course: if you find that your current company will never stop imposing these pressures on women of color, then you have to find a new table that pressures everyone equally!

There are many workplace factors that contribute to women of color questioning our worth, ability, and sense of belonging in environments that continually inflict us with moral injury and invisible perfection pressure. It's not lost on me that black and brown women also have been pressured to play up a "strong woman" narrative. At some point even the strongest people have their breaking point. And because of this narrative we don't always have the agency to speak up about how we feel or push back. On the days that I've had to show up in my combat gear to fight all the pressures, I have come to realize a very important truth—I can't do it alone, and I can't pretend these issues don't exist. Bottling up all of our moral injuries will leave us scarred for life and prevent us from securing the seat we've always worked hard to obtain. Whenever my mind set starts to waver, I remember Jay's part in the song "Empire State of Mind": "Yea, yea I'm out that

Brooklyn, now I'm down in Tribeca, right next to DeNiro, but I'll be hood forever." What if all the pressures that Jay had felt in Brooklyn caused him to give up and stop? He would have never made it to Tribeca, and we would never have had the pleasure of meeting Blue Ivy. Remember to be proud of who you are and what you bring to the table. Women of color have always been told how we should walk, talk, dress, and behave all these years due to respectability politics, and it caused many of us to lose sight of who we are and where we have come from. As I matured in my thinking, I looked at the struggles, the love, and the laughs as all of the beautiful pieces that make me who I am—even the food stamps. It's part of my story, and I wouldn't want it told any other way. It's okay to be you; we can't allow the ways of many toxic workplaces to beat us down in our mind. The next time you are faced with an Enemy State of Mind, be it self-inflicted or externally afflicted, remember you don't have to keep your feelings bottled up! You are your best advocate, and self-advocacy will be required for you to take the necessary steps to build a mindset for your growth. For me it was therapy, prayer, and a lot of Jay-Z. Securing your seat at the table will require an Empire State of Mind. The kind of mindset that takes you all the way to the top floor. The kind of mindset that, even in the desert, keeps you hydrated. We don't have to settle for a couple of pieces of shredded cheese; we can and should expect the whole enchilada at work. But first, we must see ourselves not as a snack, but as an entree.

8

NO MORE PASSES:
FOR MY WHITE READERS

I THOUGHT LONG AND hard about this chapter. I wanted to address some issues specifically for readers that might be white. It was important for me to write to white women (and white men) from a place of frustration mixed with love. I truly do love most of y'all, and I want to see us fix some of the barriers that have kept us from being on the same team. There is a lot of bad behavior that continues to follow you from generation to generation. In the workplace when bad behavior happens, an unsatisfactory employee ends up on a performance improvement plan, better known as a PIP. I am not sure how you've been able to remain on the job with such sh—y behavior. You have had way too many warnings and passes. Anyone displaying your behavior would have lost their job a long time ago. But somehow you manage to be promoted and get pay increases and awards you don't deserve. As far as I'm concerned, this is your final warning to get your sh— together. We keep trying with y'all. God knows we have every reason to cancel you for good, but we want to see the best in you. And to be fair, I have seen the best in many of you, and I am optimistic about the future!

Also, I want to give you the benefit of the doubt; maybe you've never had a woman of color as your friend. Or perhaps the one(s) you had allowed you to get away with murder and didn't nip bad behavior in the bud. I will be the first to admit, I have let several white friends get away with saying and doing sh— they had no business saying or doing. One time, I was out with some friends at a restaurant; I was probably around twenty-five. I met up with some of my childhood friends. A guy approached us and started chatting it up. Later in the conversation he asked me what I was mixed with. He was a person of color too. My white friend jumped in before I could and said, "She's just black." He snidely said, "Yes, I know, but what else are you mixed with?" She jumped in again, speaking for me, "Why do you keep asking her? She's just black; I know her parents and both of them are black." He and I just looked at each other like, *Here we go again.* We both laughed, and he schooled her on how black people can also have mixed heritage. He asked me for the third time, and I said that, on my paternal side, we are mixed with a lot of things. I remember her face like it was yesterday; she got caught with her foot in her mouth. #shedontalwaysbeknowing.

In my formative years, I laughed and let a lot of inappropriate jokes slide. For the ones under my watch, I take a little responsibility for how they now show up in the world when interacting with other people of color. Let's say this is my way of righting my wrongs. I am going to serve as the black girl-friend you never knew you needed. The one that tells you it's not okay to be dismissive to a woman of color in your staff meetings or via written correspondence. And how your pas-sive-aggressive nature sucks! I won't be shy when telling you all black people don't look alike or eat fried chicken. It's not lost on me that after reading my book, you might be shocked at the experiences women of color face in the workplace and how some white people have played a role in making it harder to as-cend. As a first step, I need your mindset to change; no longer can you run to your safe space and assume we aren't moving forward in our careers because we aren't working hard enough or aren't qualified, or that we experience the same workplace inequalities because we are both "women." Don't you hate it when men make assumptions about who you are because of your gender? The same principle applies. And the last time I checked, "assumptions" still make an ass out of people! Can I tell you how many times I've been at a store and have had white people walk up to me and assume I work there? Too many to count! The level of tone deafness is at an all-time high. We don't exist just to serve you! Again, I say this from a place of love and lots of frustration. You might not even be aware of how your actions and disposition always place us in the master/slave narrative. But let me make it clear, that's how it feels to us! And for real change to happen, you must listen and be open to unlearning what's been comfortable. Time's up, and you no longer get a hall pass for being naive and meaning well. There are some hard truths that we must address, once and for all. So let's start with some basics.

Your vocabulary. "Articulate," "angry," "hostile," "hysterical," or any other derogatory adjectives that identify us as anything besides "God's children" should no longer be used to refer to us. I was on a live Internet show, and the host said to me, "You are so articulate." I wanted to slide under my chair. And most of my friends of color pointed out that comment first, as the congratulatory messages came through—many of my white friends didn't even mention it. Do you know how many times I've heard someone tell me, "You are so articulate"? I would be a wealthy woman if I charged every time a white person said this to me. For a long time, I was so confused, like damn, what black people are you meeting if I'm wowing you? How many times has someone commented on how articulate you are? I am going to take a wild guess and say hardly never! Since we are new friends, let me tell you a secret: I've lived in the United States my entire life; my first language is English; I have a couple of degrees and an impressive résumé. Perhaps you don't interact with enough of us to know how we communicate. So that is something you need to sort out because if you interacted with more people of color, you wouldn't compliment us that way. After all you saw people of color on television in *The Jeffersons*—Weezy and George were articulate; Claire Huxtable was articulate; hell, Carl and Harriette Winslow were articulate too. I think you get my point. What is the solution? Extend your social circle to people who don't look like you. Scroll through your pictures and tell me how diverse your social circles are; this small yet impactful exercise will allow you to see your blind spots. And having just one doesn't count!

Your words are laced with microaggressions, whether you like it or not. Your words are dangerous and harmful stereotypes to bounce back from, yet you greet us with your shameful vocabulary every day at work. I know you want to defend yourself and tell me you're not being racist or projecting microaggressions, but one thing you don't get to define is what's racist and what's not. That, my friend, will put you back in hot water. And I thought we agreed you would listen and have an open mind. I know this is hard, and you probably want to call 911 on me, because that seems like one of your favorite pastimes when you are faced with a situation you dislike involving a person of color. But let me be as articulate as I can be, we are going to dig deeper into some harder topics, so I need you to toughen up. Help us change the workplace culture, starting with the words that come out of your mouth. You're an adult, so learn to filter yourself. If that's too difficult for you, remember the old saying, "If you don't have anything nice to say, don't say anything at all."

Next, let's talk hair. Workplace politics always seem to revolve around our hair. I don't know how many songs you need to hear to understand that our hair is off-limits! Hell, just keep our hair out of your mouth. Don't talk to us about our weave, especially if you aren't paying to get it installed. If you decide you want to start paying for my hair, then by all means, let's chat about it! We don't want you to talk to us about our curls, braids, or afros. Since I was in the third grade, I've had white people (men and women) touching my hair. In junior high school, there were only a few black kids at my school. Often, I was the only black student in my class. I loved my hairstyles, that is, until I went to school and kids made fun of me and called me "greaseball." Some black people use grease!

Our hair has a different texture, and some of our products could be considered moist. When they signed my yearbook, instead of calling me by my name, most white kids referred to me as Greaseball. My hair didn't look like the other kids' hair; I was made to feel different and an outsider. That feeling is reinforced when you bring those jokes and comments into the workplace. I would never comment on my colleagues' hair other than to compliment them; I would never make them feel isolated or insecure. And I would never violate them by touching their hair, unsolicited. Would you like for your colleagues to talk to you about your roots? Or point out that it's time for you to visit the salon, 'cause, those roots, girl? Wait, what if you didn't get promoted because you didn't color those roots? You would think it's pretty stupid to focus on your hairstyle and not your talent. Please give us the same courtesy? Our hair is part of who we are and our culture. It goes back to this master/slave dynamic. You think it's okay to tell women of color how to dress, how to talk, how to do their hair, down to what table is for them. We demand freedom from this basic b— level you continue to keep us at. The discourse about hair has been around for decades. I know, I know, you mean well, but hair is such a point of contention. Can *you* finally move on? Because we have been ready!

One size doesn't fit all. The word "woman" in the workplace has become a one-size-fits-all sports bra. Up until not too long ago, I bought into this "woman" phenom. It was my entry point into feminism. I loved this notion of women's rights. Then, after years in the workplace, I realized all these data points were about white women. What the hell! How can you quote statistics and keep women of color out of the conversation? As Sojourner Truth famously stated, "Ain't I a Woman?" Those stats that are often quoted refer to white women, and white women create the popular career books and platforms. Hmm, so what you're saying is that we have to settle for white women as our career advocates? Because that has served us so well? *Rolls eyes!* We can't have advocates that look like us? When I started my company, I had many white people tell me they didn't get it. Why do you need a career platform for women of color? Those conversations were clear indicators that I was on the right track. We need you to acknowledge the differences and challenges that women of color face that other women don't face. When you look at who is "winning" regarding C-Suite positions and board placements, women of color are on the lower end of every report. Lumping us into one category doesn't help us reach parity. The word "woman" is always equated to white women first, and women of color are addendums. Y'all tried to make us an addendum at the Women's March and with the Me Too movement. We are tired of being the asterisks after all your whitewashed reporting and initiatives!

I would be remiss if I didn't say that your white woman favs are not always our white woman favs. In the same way, it's not-one-size-fits-all for feminist heroes. For example, white women revere Susan B. Anthony. She did a lot of good for white women. I will not try and erase her contribution to women's history. But Susan B. Anthony was racist as hell! She was quoted as saying, "I will cut off this right arm of mine before I will ever work or demand the ballot for the Negro and not the woman." Oh, and that was her being nice. She also said, "The old anti-slavery school says women must stand back and wait until the negroes shall be recognized. But we say, if you will not give the whole loaf of suffrage to the entire people, give it to the most intelligent first. If intelligence, justice, and morality are to have precedence in the government, let the question of the woman be brought up first and that of the negro last." That is your favorite, not mine! Again, one size doesn't fit all! And PS: If you spend a little time in the history books, you will find that many of your white women favs are hella problematic.

Recently I was speaking on a panel with two other women at The Wing, an all women's coworking and social club, about salary negotiation. I was the only woman of color on the panel. The room was composed of about 90 percent white women. Each panelist gave a short introduction and a blurb about why women should ask for more. When it was my turn, I asked everyone to raise their hands if they considered themselves an ally. Just about every woman raised their hand. I said, if that's true, then as white women you must stop stating the statistic that women make X on the dollar. That number is based on white women's earnings and excludes women of color. Women of color earn significantly less than white women. I told them going forward I needed them to say that women make between Y and Z, and this is how we change the ratio. I saw it as a teachable moment. And, to my surprise, most of them seemed shocked to find out that all women don't make the same. It's small modifications to our behavior that go a long way for underrepresented groups. Sometimes we do better when we know better! And then, sometimes, history continues to repeat itself. With that said, I hope you will reconsider how you lump all women together next time you state your so-called facts.

We aren't invisible. I was riding the train a couple of months ago, and a white woman was standing next to me. She stepped on my shoes three times until I asked her to please be careful. Her response was, "I didn't see you there." She proceeded to step on my shoes two more times. I looked up and saw another white woman staring at me, wondering if I was going to check this chick. As annoyed as I was, I just didn't have the energy to check her! It's bad enough I was riding the C train. On the walk home all I could think about was how much space she was taking up and how she "didn't see me." It wasn't the first time I felt invisible, and it won't be the last. Why is it this a common theme I hear from other women of color when interacting with some white women? The idea that some white people just don't see us speaks volumes. And this wasn't an isolated situation; I've had similar experiences throughout my life. I was once told as a way of pushing back that I should take up just as much space. Not sure if this is the best advice because somebody might get hurt. I do believe that white people should be more aware of their surroundings and not feel entitled in every space they walk into (literally and figuratively)—that might allow them to see others. I am not telling you this to hurt your feelings or shame you; I am telling you so you can be aware of your disposition. My hope is that when you walk outside your house and begin your day, you take inventory of how you're engaging with people of color. We are not in a reboot of Casper the friendly ghost; we are not invisible in the workplace; we have names, we have goals, and we want more seats. And I want clean shoes! But all jokes aside, if you think back to the movie *Hidden Figures*, it wasn't that black women didn't exist; white people chose not to see them or acknowledge their contributions. And, for clarity, yes, you can physically see me, but the point I want to drive home to you is that the difference lies in acknowledging me! For so long you have chosen not to see the differences that make up our experiences, and women of color aren't here anymore to keep course-correcting you; get it together!

You need to be better success partners.

Many white men and women have been some of my biggest champions. They saw something in me and provided opportunities that allowed me to soar. But there are plenty of other black and brown women who don't have champions in the workplace. So how can you be a success partner? I use the term "success partner" because, quite frankly, I am tired of the word "ally." And I think many people are wearing this ally badge without doing anything to earn it. Being an ally means you are actively helping groups of people that are underrepresented. Since this is a career book, we need you partnering with us to provide opportunities for success. You have the power to modify the way the table looks. I need you to use your influence and modify the way boardrooms, leadership, and the wage gap look for women of color. If you currently serve in a position that would allow you to be a success partner, then use your influence. Step outside your offices, or attend an employee resource group that you don't usually frequent. Get to know the women of color in your office. When promotions come up, consider them! Half the battle is that you aren't even thinking about retaining and advancing us. Often, white people in positions of power provide opportunities to their family members, college buddies, or as part of some quid pro quo, and when that happens, usually that leaves women of color behind because we aren't in your social circles. It all goes back to a mindset: you don't consider many of us leaders because you've never seen us lead, but we rarely get the opportunity to advance into leadership roles that would demonstrate our ability to lead. Do you see how this is a recurring theme taking place across industries? If you are tired of us talking about it, be part of the solution to fix it! Being inclusive is not some hard code to crack; the remedy is simple—be intentional!

And, since I am on the topic of allyship, a.k.a. success partners, say it with me: "Success Partners." White women, some of you think you are so damn slick sometimes. Many of the most sought-after women speaking at conferences and writing books on diversity in the workplace are white women. How in the world are you going to advocate for me, present your inclusive diversity BS at the major conferences, and not have any people of color on your leadership team or in your personal life? How can you talk about diversity or how to make me feel included when you don't even have any women of color to invite to your own home? Cue Destiny's Child. No, no, no, you don't get a pass to play the advocacy hero with no receipts, and cash in on workplace oppression that many of you helped create. And to all the companies: stop putting white women who have never moved the needle for people of color on your panels to talk about subject matters that involve black or brown women. Here's a pro tip: invite black and brown women to talk about their own experiences! It's disingenuous to promote diversity, inclusion, and allyship when we are not an active part of the conversation.

Self-proclaimed allies. Another check that self-proclaimed allies do not get to cash is speaking out on matters that don't have sh— to do with them. Just because you've shown up a few times for women of color or we invited you to the family BBQ doesn't equate to saying whatever the hell you want about other women of color. I hate to play Ghost of Christmas Past, but Amber Tamblyn, white woman and self-proclaimed woke evangelist, had the nerve to call Maxine Waters out about not endorsing one of her black friends. She did this the same week Maxine Waters was receiving death threats for wanting to impeach 45. On God's green earth, if this is what you call being an ally, you, Amber Tamblyn, can keep it! With friends like you, who need enemies? And I know that she apologized and backtracked, but Amber, honey, you are far from woke if you thought that was the right move. I don't give two damns how many sorrys you say. You only backtracked because black women came for you and dragged you in true social media style. Even our most "woke" white friends must understand they still have some unlearning to do.

Which leads me to white women calling themselves woke. You found a word and you have latched onto it like your life depended on it. Other people can call you woke, but you don't get to call yourself that. I shouldn't even be calling myself that. It's lame as hell. Being woke doesn't mean you are putting in the work. Writing some enlightened essays doesn't earn you the badge. White women, where were you when Jemele Hill needed you? Where were you when London Breed needed you? How often are you there when women of color who are not famous need you? How are you showing up for us? Let's go back and look at some examples: In 2017 Amber Heard sent out this tweet, "Just heard there's an ICE checkpoint in Hollywood, a few blocks from where I live. Everyone better give their housekeepers, nannies and landscapers a ride home tonight." In that same year, Scarlett Johansson made some insensitive remarks surrounding a trans role she eventually withdrew from. And Sally Kohn found herself in a showdown on Twitter with Call Your Girlfriend podcast host Aminatou Sow after Kohn misquoted Sow in her book. White women like Amber Heard, Scarlett Johansson, and Sally Kohn sometimes get too comfortable and forget advocacy isn't a punch-card system. When you get enough punches for doing good, you don't get inducted into the honorary club—to school people and call stuff out like a woman of color. As Beyoncé and Jay-Z said, "Have you ever seen a crowd go apesh—?" And in Sally's case, we saw the internet go apesh— as she battled black women during her book launch. Time and time again y'all muck it up. I am starting to question if self-awareness will meet you at the church altar, but then again, I am an optimist!

And this, my friend, is The Memo. We can't be successful without being on the same team. I applaud you for reading this book, because part of being a success partner is owning some of your behavior and listening to our stories. You can't sit back with your white friends talking about what people of color need if you haven't spent time listening to our stories. It's not about shaming or making you feel guilty; it's about educating you on how to best level the playing field. What you should and shouldn't say and the lessons you have been taught for decades that seem not to be getting through to you. Oddly enough, back in high school I was a hall monitor and had the ability to give out hall passes, but those days are long gone. There are no more passes to give out. And as Heidi Klum so concisely put it on several seasons of *Project Runway*, "You're either in or you're out." And as your new friend, I can't wait to see some improvements on your PIP.

9

SAY MY NAME, SAY MY NAME

WOMEN OF COLOR, from Sacagawea to Harriet Tubman to Dolores Huerta and Flo Kennedy and Pramila Jayapal, have been leaders throughout history. We've never needed an invitation to take on a leadership role. And even when our invitation was lost in the mail, we shaped any room we walked into. We honor the women that have blazed trails and allowed us the privilege of not having to fight as hard to achieve equality. These women have fought discrimination, violence, and barriers to education while being excluded from working in certain occupations. Audre Lorde said, "There is no hierarchy of oppressions." And we say the names of women from the past and present that don't always receive an award or trophy for opening up doors for the next woman of color.

Contrary to popular belief, there are black and brown women in leadership roles at some of the most well-known companies in the world; the problem is we don't know their names. Why? Often the women in business that we hear and read about are not women of color. Did you know that Edith Cooper was the most senior black woman at Goldman Sachs before she retired in 2017? Why isn't Edith as well-known as Marissa Mayer? Ursula Burns was the first black woman CEO of a Fortune 500 company (and so far the only). She is an icon, yet most people only know of Sheryl Sandberg and Meg Whitman. One thing is certain—black and brown women aren't taking up the leadership pages of Fortune 500 companies, but we are in these spaces. And if other women of color want to see women that look like them in high-profile positions, they need to know they exist. For so long I used to think that we might not be working as hard or might not aspire for more, because I would only read about and see white women in the business magazines. But again, this is the lie "they" would like us to believe. I called this chapter "Say My Name, Say My Name" because there are women of color that you should know about are working hard in a variety of industries. I don't want to sound like a broken record, but representation is important, and if you see women who look like you, who secured the seat at the levels that you aspire to, or if you're at this level and often feel like a unicorn, you can gain strength from knowing there are others. The women of color that appear on our favorite television shows shouldn't be our only role models. Our role models should be diverse, but unfortunately, many leadership pages of companies and organizations don't reflect that.

Women like Patricia Roberts Harris, who was the first African American woman to hold a corporate board seat (IBM). She was also the first African American woman to serve in the US cabinet under President Jimmy Carter. Did you know that Simone Askew is the first black woman to lead the West Point Corps of Cadets? There are many women you should know about, but I don't have enough pages to tell you about all their contributions. I decided to pull a list of black and brown women crushing glass in the workplace. They are women I recently discovered, and I will need your help to continue adding names to this list of badass women! The more women we identify, the more others will learn and acknowledge our contributions to the workforce. It's awesome to be the first one, but they shouldn't be the last ones. We are not only educated but also more than capable of leading organizations across the spectrum, from corporations to nonprofits. My hope is that this list inspires you and that one day we can add your name if that's the way you want your story written. Most importantly, use these women as mission fuel as you climb your ladder of success! There's no doubt that many of these Super Sheros went through experiences similar to ours, but they pushed forward and didn't back down! You should know the following women and support and amplify their work in business:

- **Suzanne Shank** is the chairwoman and CEO at Siebert, Cisneros, Shank, and Company, which she established in 1996. Suzanne started working on Wall Street in 1987. She has been named one of the top twenty-five women in finance. She's also been named one of Wharton School's 125 Top Influential People.

- **Katrina Adams** is the chairman of the board and intermediate past president at the US Tennis Association.

Katrina is the first African American to hold this title in the organization's 135-year history.

- **Tracey Travis** is the executive vice president and chief financial officer at the Estée Lauder Companies. Prior to joining Estée Lauder, Tracey was the CFO at Ralph Lauren.

- **Rhea Combs** is the museum curator at the Smithsonian National Museum of African American History. Rhea also holds a PhD from Emory University.

- **Alicia Boler Davis** is the executive vice president of global manufacturing and labor relations at General Motors. Alicia was also named Black Engineer of the Year in 2018. Additionally, she holds a board seat at General Mills.

- **Melody Birmingham-Byrd** is senior vice president and chief procurement officer for Duke Energy. She was previously president of Duke Energy's Indiana operations, where the electric utility company was the state's largest.

- **Channing Dungey** is the vice president of content at Netflix. In Channing's former role, she was the first African American president of the ABC Entertainment Group. She has a long history of being a champion of diversity and inclusion.

- **Sheena Wright** is president of United Way of New York City and the first woman to lead the nonprofit in its history. She was formerly CEO of the Abyssinian Development Corporation.

- **Bonita Stewart** is the vice president of global partnerships at Google. An alumna of Howard University and Harvard Business School, *AdAge* named her a *Woman to Watch* in 2011.

- **Christine Simmons** is COO at the Academy of Motion Pictures. Prior to that she was the President and COO of the Los Angeles Sparks.

- **Jo Ann Jenkins** is CEO at the American Association of Retired Persons. She has been recognized by *Black Enterprise* as one of the most powerful women in business.

- **Anjali Sud** is CEO at Vimeo. Prior to joining Vimeo, she worked at Amazon and Time Warner.

- **Susan Chapman Hughes** is the executive vice president and global head of digital capabilities, transformation, and operations at American Express. Susan also serves on the board at Potbelly Sandwich Works.

- **Silvia Lagnado** is the executive vice president and global chief marketing officer at McDonald's. *AdAge* named her one of the 100 influential women in advertising in 2012.

- **Sheryl Adkins-Green** is the chief marketing officer at Mary Kay and the president. She was the recipient of the 2012 Global Marketer Award by the Academy of Marketing Science.

- **Teresa L. White** is the president of Aflac United States. She received the Distinguished Alumni Award from the University of Texas at Arlington.

- **Leilani M. Brown** is the senior vice president of strategic partnerships and external engagement for K12, Inc. She is the author of *From Campus to Cubicle: 25 Professional Tips for Your First Professional Year* and serves on the board at Middlebury College.

- **Ivy McGregor** is the director of philanthropy and corporate relations at Parkwood Entertainment. She also serves as an adjunct professor at Howard University.

- **Soraya Coley** is the president of California State Polytechnic University at Pomona. She is the first woman to be named president of that institution. She is also a member of the Los Angeles Chamber of Commerce.

- **Della Britton Baeza** is president and chief executive officer of the Jackie Robinson Foundation. Prior to joining JRF, Della was an entertainment industry executive. She helped launch the career of pop sensation Ashanti. She is a graduate of Princeton University and Columbia Law School.

- **Jerri DeVard** is executive vice president and chief customer officer at Office Depot. Prior to joining Office Depot, she was an executive at ADT. She is also on the board at Cars.com and Under Armour.

- **Caroline Clarke** is chief brand officer for *Women of Power* at *Black Enterprise* magazine. She cofounded the largest executive conference for women of color, called the Women of Power Summit. Clarke is an author and award-winning journalist.

- **Radhika Jones** is editor in chief of *Vanity Fair* magazine. She is the first Indian-origin person, and person of color, to serve as editor in chief in the magazine's history. Prior to joining *Vanity Fair*, she spent time at the *New York Times* and *Time* magazine.

- **Lisa Wardell** is chief executive officer and president of Adtalem Global Education Group. She is the only African American woman who is CEO at a Fortune 1000 company. She holds degrees from Vassar and Stanford Law School.

- **Katrina Jones** is the head of diversity and inclusion at Twitch, the first person to hold that title there. Previously, she worked at Accenture in the global diversity and inclusion department.

- **Esi Eggleston Bracey** is the executive vice president and chief operating officer at Unilever. She was previously the president of consumer beauty at Coty.

- **Telisa Yancy** is the COO at American Family Insurance. She was named to the prestigious Ebony Power 100 List in 2016. She also holds degrees from the University of Illinois and Northwestern University's Kellogg School of Business.

- **Connie Lindsey** is Northern Trust's Executive Vice President and Head of Corporate Social Responsibility and Global Diversity and Inclusion. She served as National Board President of Girl Scouts of the USA. Lindsey received her BA in Finance from the University of Wisconsin–Milwaukee and has completed the Harvard Business School Executive Education Corporate Social Responsibility program. Connie was recognized with the 2017 Women of Influence Award by Chicago Business Journal.

- **Thelma Golden** is the director and chief curator at the Studio Museum in Harlem. She is also on the board at the Barack Obama Foundation.

- **Barbara Whye** is the vice president of human resources and chief diversity and inclusion officer at Intel. In 2014, she was awarded the National Society of Black Engineers Career Excellence Award.

I would be remiss if I didn't mention the names of women who also blazed trails in business whom you have probably heard of; I will continue to sing their praises: Oprah Winfrey, Debra Lee, Mellody Hobson, Rosalind Brewer, Carla Harris, Desiree Rogers, Janice Bryant Howroyd, Linda Johnson Rice, Ann-Marie Campbell, and Ann Fudge. It takes all hands on deck to have no ceilings!

It's important that we say their names because we don't want our contributions erased from history. Even if the top magazines don't showcase them, we have the ability to lift up and amplify the voices of our own mavericks. Thank God for social media and the power of lifting our voices. You can search any social media feed and find the hashtags #blackwomenlead, #trustblackwomen, #listentoblackwomen, and #blackwomenatwork. Even in politics, women of color fight the systemic barriers of having a seat at the table. I spent half of my childhood in California and Illinois, and I remember when Carol Moseley Braun was elected to the Senate in 1992 as the first African American woman senator. I was too young to understand the significance of this, but the challenges that face black and brown women in our government became quite clear, because we didn't see our next black woman senator until 2016, when Kamala Harris was elected. Thank God for our godmother Shirley Chisholm for paving the way not just for black women, but black men too. In 1972, Shirley Chisholm was the first black female candidate for a major party's nomination for the presidency of the United States. She met a lot of resistance; even the women's movement didn't back her candidacy. Such revered white feminists as Gloria Steinem chose to back a white man instead. Shirley Chisholm once said, in a speech she gave at Howard University in 1969, "I intend to stay here and fight because the blood, sweat, and tears of our forefathers are rooted in the soil of this country. And the reason that Wall Street is the great financial center that it is today is because of the blood, sweat, and tears of your forefathers who worked in the tobacco and the cotton fields." And because of her standing and fighting, we now see a record number of women of color running for office and getting elected. Some cities in the United States are seeing their first African American women as mayors: London Breed in San Francisco, LaToya Cantrell in New Orleans, and Vi Lyles in Charlotte, North Carolina. And the first Native American women elected to Congress—Sharice Davids and Deb Haaland. There are hundreds of women of color serving as elected officials in state legislatures. And several black women serve in the US Congress. Countless black women labor as public servants. We belong in every room we walk into, from Wall Street to entertainment studios to legislatures. And we will continue to add to this list and Say Their Names!

10

LET'S WERK

ONE OF THE most annoying things about some people that make it to the top is that they don't always share their secret sauce. I never understood how some men or women who could use their influence to help others advance choose not to. Margaret Thatcher said there is a special place in hell for women who don't support other women. Actually, I think there must be an additional torture chamber for women of color who don't help each other because we all know how hard the fight is. Over the course of starting The Memo, I have met some of the most influential women of color, and many of them chose to pat me on the back and say "Good work" and shut the door on me. They were black women whom I had high expectations for, those I looked up to because publicly they stated they were for the advancement of other women of color. They claimed they wanted to bring more people of color with them, but in real life, they were only looking out for themselves. It was a hard pill to swallow, and to be honest, it still bothers me. With the little influence I have, I am trying to do the best I can; yet they have the world at their fingertips and choose to do nothing.

Then before I drowned at my pity party, I snapped out of it and realized that I didn't want women like them fighting alongside of me anyway. The good news is there are way more black and brown women who have opened the door for me or have thrown me a bone than those who haven't. I have been fortunate to have met some amazing black and brown women who have been helpful: Tiffany Dufu, author of *Drop the Ball*, and Keisha Smith-Jeremie, founder of Sania Applesauce. They don't subscribe to the "only one" syndrome, this idea that there can't be more than one of us winning. In my opinion, this syndrome isn't something we can completely blame white people for; that ideology is very much alive in people of color as well. And this is the part in the book where I tell you to cut that mess out. We should all be helping each other get a leg up. I am not saying don't be cautious about who you assist, but don't hoard the goods for yourself. I wrote this book for a couple of reasons: (1) If you didn't have the access and information, you have it now, and (2) If you need some additional resources in your tool kit, I hope you can pick up an additional few in this chapter. I want to share with you the resources I use and templates that have helped me along the way. As Paula Abdul would say on *American Idol*, "Make it your own." And remember, investing in yourself is your responsibility; you can't expect anyone else to do that for you! Here are my cheat codes . . . enjoy.

Assessments and Tests

1. **Personality Tests**: If you aspire to lead a team or engage effectively with your colleagues, I think it's important to understand your personality type and how you can best engage with other personality types within the workplace. Knowing your personality type will help you maximize your skills and talents. A good first place to start is the Myers-Briggs Personality Test. (Side note: I think this is a good test for relationships as well.) According to this test, there are sixteen personality types. Another one I have taken is the DISC Assessment, which describes four personality types.

2. **Assessments:** We all have a different set of strengths. I would encourage you to take the Clifton Strengths Assessment. I live by this test! Any chance I get to recommend it, I do! Many of us already know our weakness, but if we better understood our strengths, then we could do a better job of leveraging them in the workplace. After the test, you are provided with reports and resources to help you develop strengths you didn't even realize could be assets. Another recommendation is taking an emotional intelligence assessment. Emotional intelligence covers everything from how people manage their behavior to how they interact with others to their decision-making process. One book that has helped me is *Emotional*

Intelligence 2.0, which discusses relationship management and self-awareness, among other things, based on a research sample of more than 500,000 people. This book also includes a test. Many companies are starting to incorporate emotional intelligence assessments into their hiring processes.

Your Salary

As Beyoncé said, "The best revenge is your paper." So make sure you are leaving nothing on the table, from your salary to fringe benefits. Here I list three women of color who can help you move closer to your negotiation goals:

- Jamie Lee is a negotiation and leadership coach. She also has a podcast to help you crack the code on negotiation strategies. Learn more about Jamie at http://www.jamieleecoach.com/.

- Tanya Tarr is a *Forbes* contributor and negotiation strategist. Tanya also hosts regular webinars on negotiation strategies. Connect with Tanya at http://youredgecoaching.com/.

- Jacqueline Twillie is on a mission to eliminate the gender wage gap. She is the founder of ZeroGap. To connect with Jacqueline, go to https://www.jacquelinetwillie.com.

Résumé Tips

I am going to assume you have put together a professional résumé and also that you know about margins, fonts, and consistency (dates, font size, outdated information, and experience).

Dos:

1. Tell your career story. It's up to you to articulate your skills and achievements. If you have been out of college for over five years, you don't have to include your old jobs or internships. By now you have experience that should be able to stand on its own.

2. Include a professional statement. This is not the same as an objective statement. Most hiring managers will glance at your résumé to see if it contains what they are looking for. Create a statement that mirrors an elevator pitch so the recruiter will want to review the rest.

3. Read through the job description. Make sure your résumé reflects what the position is seeking. The language they use should also be incorporated into your résumé (career story). I don't think most applicants read through job descriptions as thoroughly as they should.

4. Highlight relevant experiences and projects. You don't have to make a laundry list—just provide the most impactful.

5. Keep your résumé current and ready. You never know when it will be time to shoot your shot. What if your dream job is presented to you and you only have three minutes to provide a résumé? If you haven't updated your résumé in years, then you might miss out on the chance of a lifetime. Additionally, you might have forgotten some of your achievements to highlight. Stay ready!

Don'ts:

1. Avoid listing old skills or skills that most people have as well. For example, "I am proficient in Microsoft Office," which we talked about earlier. Come on, man! Most people are proficient in Microsoft, the Internet, and so on. If you kill it in Excel, then be specific: "I know how to make pivot tables for X or specialize in creating formulas." I can't emphasize enough the power of being specific.

2. That point in number 1 is so true it bears repeating: don't use vague language. Be specific about what your former jobs entailed.

3. Don't use the same résumé for everything that you apply for. Make sure you have a few different versions.

4. Don't apply just to be applying. Make sure you're being intentional about the jobs you are applying for. Apply to jobs that you are interested in. We spend a good chunk of our time at work, so don't apply to places where you know you don't want to work. You owe that to yourself. Also, you can reach out to someone at the companies that interest you and set up an informational interview. This will allow you to find out the ins and outs before you commit to the interview process.

5. Don't use "I" or "me." For example, don't say "I am a team player" or "I am a hard worker." Be careful with overusing words. It's better to demonstrate how you're a team player by giving an example. At this stage of your career, it's assumed that everyone is a hard worker and a team player. That doesn't make you stand out!

Email Templates

I was rewatching the 1999 movie *Cruel Intentions* with Reese Witherspoon, Sarah Michelle Gellar, and Ryan Phillippe, and in one conversation between his character Sebastian and Sarah's character Kathryn, he said, "Emails are for geeks."

It's almost laughable to think about that statement ten years later; boy, was Sebastian wrong! If you're not spending most of your time communicating electronically, then you're probably missing out on building your social capital. And because most people receive numerous emails every hour, correspondence can be a tricky thing. You want to craft and send messages that will stand out and inspire the recipients to respond. Here are a few sample templates to use when reaching out to people; please make them your own!

Reaching Out / First Contact

Reaching out to a stranger can be tough, but remember you are your best advocate and the only way to get in front of your goals is to put yourself out there. Here is a sample template requesting a meeting:

Hi, Irma,

I hope this message finds you well. My name is Minda Harts, and I'm a social impact entrepreneur helping the next generation of women of color advance in the workplace. I created a digital career education platform company called The Memo that helps hundreds of black and brown women prepare for their seat at the table via our career boot camps. I also have a podcast called Secure the Seat. And next spring my debut nonfiction book, *The Memo*, which discusses what it's like to "lean in" as a woman of color in the workplace, will be published by Hachette Book Group.

I live in NYC and have been spending more time in the LA area while working on my book. I am inspired by the work that you do in your community and would love the opportunity to connect with you and brainstorm on ways I might be able to support women of color in LA or find out if you know anyone who might be interested in my work. Would you be available for an initial phone meeting the first week of June?

Thank you for your consideration.

With gratitude,

Xx

Follow Up

After you've had your meeting, you want to make sure you follow up on the items that you discussed. Below you will see a sample email that I sent twenty-four hours after a meeting. I made it easy for them to copy and paste or forward items along. Please make things easy on the person that offers to help you out.

Hi, Kevin,

So good to catch up with you this week. Thank you for always making time for me—it means more than you know. I left feeling like I could keep the train moving forward. Below are the follow-up items we discussed. I know you have tons on your plate; feel free to make introductions when you can. Also, I attached our Women of Resilience Awards sponsorship deck.

ABC Company and The Memo Event:

A dialogue between black men and women. I think we should plan for the summer or fall of 2018. I see this being a well-curated panel discussion between black men and black women in which we center our talking points around topics that we can discuss in a meaningful way—to help us bridge the gap, and to provide solid, actionable steps that each person can leave with to be better advocates. #fortheculture

I think it would be cool to have panelists like James Doe, Cindy Doe, Asa Doe, and Beverly Doe from your community. I see it even being broken into a couple of panels. Maybe a half-day luncheon. Just brainstorming.

Foundation Intros:
American Express Foundation
Ford Foundation

Introductions to Black Women:
Jane Doe
Dina Doe
Carla Doe
Anita Doe

A blurb about me and The Memo to pass along:
Minda Harts is a social impact entrepreneur helping the next generation of women of color advance in the workplace. She created a digital career education platform company called The Memo that helps hundreds of black and brown women prepare for their seat at the table via their career boot camps. Next spring she will debut her nonfiction book, *The Memo*, which discusses what it's like

to "lean in" as a woman of color in the workplace and will be published by Hachette Book Group. **Her Press Kit (clickable link).**

Thank you,
Xx

Touching Base / Reconnecting

Here is a template to help you reconnect with someone you haven't been in touch with for some time. I think it's a good best practice to touch base with people you want to keep in the loop about your work and not drop off their radar.

Hi, Michael,

How are you? I hope this email finds you well. A little over a year ago, our mutual friend Gabe introduced us. You were so kind to connect with me and learn about my business The Memo. I wanted to give you an update.

1) The Memo is doing well. We have some case studies that show success among some of our members.

2) We have received press coverage in *Forbes*, HuffPost, *The Guardian*, NBC News, and *Black Enterprise* magazine.

3) We received an Angel Investment (seed capital).

Thank you for your support and encouragement. Over the last year, I am becoming a new voice in the conversation around advancing women of color in the workplace. I have hustled like crazy since we last spoke, yet there is still a lot of ground to cover. I wanted you to know I am still moving forward. I hope to have you speak to our members in the near future.

Have a great summer!

With gratitude,

Xx

PS: *Wonder Woman* was awesome!

Thank-You Messages

Never forget to thank someone who made a connection for you and also make them aware that you are going to meet or had the meeting with the person they introduced you to. This is a pro tip in relationship building. Keeping them in the loop signals that you can be trusted with their social capital. Here is a simple yet impactful thank-you message:

Hey, Jalen,

Hope you are well. Congrats again on your baby girl. Just wanted to let you know I am meeting with Larry in Chicago next Wednesday. Thank you for making that connection.

Have a good night.

Xx

Introducing Contact and Connections

The new normal in introducing people to one another is that both people must opt in beforehand. You don't want to assume that someone wants to make the connection. And as well-intentioned as you might be in connecting two cool people, you first want to separately ask each person if it's okay to make the introduction. Once they have both agreed, then you make the introduction. Personally, I am not bothered by people who make connections between me and someone they think I should know, yet you should be aware of the new etiquette of double opt-in introductions. Here are two samples after the double opt-in introduction was made:

Intro 1:

Minda,

Janet is the brilliant lady behind the ABC Women T-shirts you see everywhere (which benefit a number of fantastic female-focused causes). And Minda is the founder of The Memo, the career site that focuses on woc. I was telling Janet about The Memo and thought you two should know each other. Go forth and take over the world.

Xo

Intro 2:

Minda,

Please meet my friend Kasey. She's currently at CNN (based in NYC) after spending some time at the *LA Times* and Atlantic Media Company, among other places. As "folks in media" go, she's among the most well regarded in terms of using digital for storytelling and also for her efforts to diversify newsrooms.

Kasey, as noted, I met Minda Harts and learned about her org, The Memo, as a coach in the CivicX Accelerator put on by Points of Light. Her work struck me as both necessary and super practical, which gives me optimism for their impact moving forward.

I'm pretty sure you can take it from here, but if I can be of any further help, don't hesitate in reaching out. To paraphrase Kanye, you're both dope and you do dope (ish).

Hugs,

Xx

Pitching Your Brand

Many of you are building your brand and looking to garner press or increase your speaking engagements. Often, this requires you to pitch yourself to media outlets or conferences. Here is a sample pitch:

Hi, PR Company,

My name is Minda Harts, and I founded The Memo, a digital career platform that helps put more women of color in the C-Suite. In my X years in corporate America, I found that career development is not created equal and career advancement advice often over-represents the experiences of white women climbing the ladder. I felt as though many of the career platforms like ⎯⎯⎯⎯, ⎯⎯⎯⎯, and ⎯⎯⎯⎯, to name a few, focused on providing one-size-fits-all solutions for women. On October 17 there was an article on your platform titled ⎯⎯⎯⎯. The article discussed the challenges we face but didn't offer tangible tools to combat them.

Who is going to break the "black" glass ceiling? Who is going to be our Sheryl Sandberg and help lead the cavalry for black and brown women to lean in and not out because our employers are not investing in our development? If we all leave to start our own companies, there won't be any-one inside these companies that look like us—some of us should stay and create change!

I started my company because I wanted to help solve this problem, to provide tools built for us, by us. With less than 4 percent of women of color in the C-Suite of Fortune 500 companies, I realized we need mechanisms in place to help advance and retain women of color. We launched our career products in the summer of 2016 and have over ⎯⎯⎯ women of color on our platform and grow-ing. They are investing in themselves, and now we are of-fering our digital products to companies so they can invest in the retention and advancement of their diverse talent. I want women of color to know there are tables with their names on them, and The Memo is here to help. Please find additional information about me and a short video here (clickable link). After reading your recent articles on black women in the workplace, I thought this pitch would be appropriate. Thank you for your time, and I hope to hear from you in the future.

With gratitude,

Xx

Professional Development Conferences

Many of us are looking to build our network and connect with like-minded women. I would suggest investing in yourself by attending one or two conferences a year to stay in the loop and build your network. Side note: Your company or organization might have a professional development stipend to help assist you with attending one or more of these annual conferences.

- Black Enterprise Women of Power Summit

- ColorComm

- Forbes Women Summit

- National Urban League Conference

- National Association of Black Journalists

Professional Development Platforms

In addition to occasional professional development conferences, you might need weekly, monthly, or quarterly trainings and a community of women to help you stay accountable to your career development trajectory. Another part of investing in yourself is investing in courses and a community to help you grow. Think of your career like a streaming platform: you might not use your streaming service every day, but it's there when you need it. I suggest utilizing career development platforms to help you stay ready and supported during the wins and the obstacles.

- The Memo, www.myweeklymemo.com

- Ellevate, www.ellevate.com

- Black Career Women's Network, www.bcwnetwork.com/

- The Latinista, www.thelatinista.com

- The Cru, www.findyourcru.com

Career Coaches

Often, I hear women say they can't afford a career coach, but soon after they will run over to their favorite Nike location and buy the new cross-trainer shoes and a hoodie to match. Many of us have not been educated about or introduced to the power of a career coach. Most of the top executives have hired a career coach to help them get to the next level. How badly do you want to level up? Here are the names of three career coaches to help you reach that next level.

- Arquella Hargrove offers three-month, six-month, and twelve-month coaching packages to help you become the leader you were meant to be. Learn more about Arquella at http://arquellahargrove.com.

- Kanika Tolver specializes in career pivots and how to find a job that's the right fit for you. Learn more about Kanika at https://kanikatolver.com.

- Tiffany F. Southerland helps her clients get clear about their personal and professional strengths and how to leverage those strengths. To connect with Tiffany go to http://www.fourcornerscoach.com.

Podcasts

If you hadn't guessed, I love to invest in myself. I use resources that require a monetary investment and that are easy to access. When I don't have enough money to invest in a career coach or buy a new webinar, I listen to career-related and inspirational podcasts. Here are six podcasts that are part of my weekly career development routine. I hope you will add them to your lineup and share with others:

- Secure the Seat, hosted by Minda Harts

- Trailblazer's Podcast, hosted by Stephen A. Hart

- Beyond the Business Suit, hosted by Kailei Carr

- The Great Girlfriends, hosted by Sybil Amuti and Brandice Daniel

- Le Vital Corp Salon, hosted by Kara Snyder

- Schoolin' Life, hosted by Ashley and Marcy

Diversity and Inclusion

- The Factuality Game is a ninety-minute crash course on structural inequality in America. Go to www.fac tualitythegame.com.

- Multicultural Insights provides multicultural market research and strategy at https://www.mc-insights.com.

The Women of Color Equity Initiative

In the fall of 2018, I launched The Women of Color Equity Initiative. I am continuously thinking about ways to bridge the gap between entry-level roles and management roles. Around 11 percent of women of color hold a managerial position, less than 8 percent hold a senior managerial role, and less than 4 percent are in the C-Suite. Given the high number of edu-cated women of color in the United States, there's no logical reason why women of color do not occupy more of these roles. Each week, I have companies reach out to me and ask if I know a woman of color who might be interested in a particular position, and now I want companies to be able to connect with you directly!

We can no longer accept the false narrative of a faulty pipeline issue when it's the lack of opportunity. No matter how many professional development courses or conferences you attend, it won't matter if you don't have *access*, *opportunity*, and *equity*! I have created The Women of Color Equity Initiative to help close the gap between women of color and those who identify as women of color and the roles that we aren't actively recruited to occupy and secure.

The Women of Color Equity Initiative aims to increase the number of women of color in management and C-Suite roles in corporate and not-for-profit work. While many women of color are opting to leave the traditional workplace and become entrepreneurs, many want to continue to advance their careers in a more conventional setting, and we need to invest in their success as well.

The Women of Color Equity Initiative (A Sourcing Tool) achieves this by connecting professionals with companies and organizations that want to recruit and retain women of color to enter a healthy, inclusive, and equitable work environment. My hope is that this initiative will help increase the number of women of color advancing into management and senior roles in the workplace across industries by winter 2019. You have worked too hard to turn back now!

If you are interested in participating in this initiative or know someone who is, go to www.mindaharts.com and join our searchable database so companies and organizations can connect with you for your next leadership role. Anyone who is dedicated to supporting the advancement of women of color in the workplace is welcome! This initiative does not discriminate with regard to age. We need all hands on deck!

ACKNOWLEDGMENTS

GOD (JESUS AND HOLY SPIRIT), you knew me before I stepped foot on this earth. You birthed a purpose inside me that I feel privileged to execute. Thank you for trusting me as your feet on the ground. To my guardian angels that are no longer with me, even though I feel your energy every day—Granny Pearl, Deirdre (Big Sis), Liz (SD for life), and Jeremiah (my little warrior)—I wish I could share this moment with you on earth. To my mom, thank you for pushing me through this process, even when I doubted myself and my calling. Nothing like a mother's love; thank you. Dad, thank you for your love and support. Gabe, Michael, Sonia, and Jumbo, thank you for your encouragement and love. Miranda, where do I even start? You helped me tap into parts of our culture that I didn't even know I needed—not to mention that I don't think I could have finished writing this book without you—thank you for your love and support. Stephen, you are my brother from another mother—thank you for the pushes and love. Shawn, thank you for always being my silent partner and mentor. To Lauren, thank you for your love and support—they finally got The Memo! Ben and Christine—so much love for you and your family, thank you! Thank you, Barry E. —you have always believed in my vision. Thank you, Linda T. for your friendship and encouragement. Matt, thank you for your investment; you are the best at tough love. To my Granny Irma—thank you for being a strong black woman. To your four daughters, Aunt Nako, Aunt G, Aunt Kasey, and Aunt Arnetta, thank you for allowing me to be like the sixth sister. To my grandparents, aunts, uncles, cousin Demetra, spiritual brothers/sisters, cousins, and those I consider part of my family—thank you. My godsons, Nupers and Birds—love y'all! To Monica, we became Soul Sisters before the signatures were even dry. Thank you for making a dream come true and finding the right home for this book—you are the best agent! The team at Liza Dawson Associates: thank you! The team at Hachette Book Group and Seal Press: thank you! To Stephanie: thank you for taking a chance on a first-time author who is super passionate about women of color at work. This book wouldn't exist without you. To Kara and Justin: from our early talks, you helped get this book ball rolling—thank you. Thank you to all my friends who checked in on me and pushed me, too many of you to name—it's all love (but s/o to my girls for life: Ama, Kim, Ta'nia, and Christine)! Natashia Deon: thank you for a seat at your table. Tiffany Dufu: I don't even have the words to express my gratitude—I appreciate you more than you will ever know. To all my mentors who gave me advice along my career journey—thank you. Pastor K, Harlem world! Thank you for your prayers and accountability. To all the people that I have met along my path: thank you for depositing life lessons along the way. Annette: thank you for always rooting for me all the way from Canada. To Jamie, my other SD, always and forever! To all the women of color out there— I love each and every one of you; thank you for allowing me to share this book with you! To my ancestors: thank you for allowing me to be your wildest dreams; your struggle was not in vain. To Beyoncé and Jay-Z: we don't even know one another, but your talents and the way you show generosity to the world continue to inspire me; respect! To Sarah Jakes Roberts: your sermons got me through this entire book—thank you. To the strong black and brown women who have been fighting for equality—you are the MVPs. To those I asked to blurb for me and you said yes—thank you! To those who are my social media friends: y'all go hard for me and I have so much love for you. To The Memo community: you helped me find my place in this world, and I am forever grateful to all that have supported the journey! And, last but not least, Boston, you give me life. Mommy loves you.

INDEX

ABOUT THE AUTHOR

MINDA HARTS is a well-connected, sought-after speaker, and thought-leader, frequently speaking on topics of advancing women of color, leadership, diversity, and entrepreneurship. In 2018, Minda was named as one of 25 Emerging Innovators by American Express. Minda is an assistant professor of public service of NYU's Robert F. Wagner Graduate School of Public Service and the founder of The Memo LLC, a career development company for women of color. Minda was also chosen by General Assembly to serve as one of their Dream Mentors, alongside women like Cindy Gallop. *Secure the Seat* is her weekly career podcast for women of color. Minda is originally from Southern California and currently resides in New York City.